Ruth Hubbard and Gilles Paquet

Probing the Bureaucratic Mind

About Canadian Federal Executives

| Collaborative Decentred Metagovernance Series

This series of books is designed to define cumulatively the contours of collaborative decentred metagovernance. At this time, there is still no canonical version of this paradigm: it is *en émergence*. This series intends to be one of many 'construction sites' to experiment with various dimensions of an effective and practical version of this new approach.

Metagovernance is the art of combining different forms or styles of governance, experimented with in the private, public and social sectors, to ensure effective coordination when power, resources and information are widely distributed, and the governing is of necessity decentred and collaborative.

The series invites conceptual and practical contributions focused on different issue domains, policy fields, *causes célèbres*, functional processes, etc. to the extent that they contribute to sharpening the new apparatus associated with collaborative decentred metagovernance.

In the last few decades, there has been a need felt for a more sophisticated understanding of the governing of the private, public and social sectors: for less compartmentalization among sectors that have much in common; and for new conceptual tools to suggest new relevant questions and new ways to carry out the business of governing, by creatively recombining the tools of governance that have proven successful in all these sectors. These efforts have generated experiments that have been sufficiently rich and wide-ranging in the various laboratories to warrant efforts to pull together what we know at this stage.

This sixth book in the series reports on conversations with a large sample of senior executives in the Canadian federal public service. We attempted to probe their way of tackling progressively more and more difficult problems in order to gain a sense of the weaknesses that these conversations revealed about the capabilities of the federal public service to respond to current challenges, and of what might be done to kick start a process of refurbishment of these capabilities.

Interested parties are invited to join the Chautauqua.

– Editorial Board

Other titles published by INVENIRE are listed at the end of this book.

Ruth Hubbard and Gilles Paquet

Probing the Bureaucratic Mind

About Canadian Federal Executives

INVENIRE

Ottawa, Canada

2014

Invenire © 2014

Library and Archives Canada Cataloguing in Publication

Hubbard, Ruth, 1942-, author
    Probing the bureaucratic mind : about Canadian federal
executives / Ruth Hubbard and Gilles Paquet.

Includes bibliographical references.
Issued in print and electronic formats.
ISBN 978-1-927465-12-7 (pbk.).--ISBN 978-1-927465-13-4 (html)

        1. Government executives--Canada. 2. Government executives--
Canada--Attitudes. 3. Civil service--Canada. 4. Critical thinking--Canada.
5. Problem solving--Canada. 6. Learning ability. I. Paquet, Gilles, 1936-,
author II. Title.

JL111.E93H83 2014   352.3'90971   C2014-901134-2
                                                        C2014-901135-0

Invenire would like to gratefully acknowledge the ongoing support for this
series by the Centre on Governance, University of Ottawa.

Published by Invenire
P.O. Box 87001
Ottawa, Canada K2P 1X0
www.invenire.ca

Cover design by Sandy Lynch
Layout and design by Sandy Lynch
Printed in Canada by Imprimerie Gauvin

Distributed by:
Commoners' Publishing
631 Tubman Cr.
Ottawa, Canada K1V 8L6
Tel.: 613-523-2444
Fax: 888-613-0329
sales@commonerspublishing.com
www.commonerspublishing.com

Table of Contents

Introduction 1
Beyond the traditional *clichés*. 4
The rise of network governance 5
The federal bureaucracy under siege 8
The process. 10
The outcome: probing a mindset 12

Chapter 1 Cat's cradling:
the capacity to cope 17
A syncretic view of each theme discussed 18
Contextual issues 18
Diversity 18
Security. 20
Ethics. 22
Disloyalty 25
Organizational culture and new governance tools. . . . 27
Corporate culture 27
The Gomery world 29
Public-private partnerships. 32
Partitioning anew the federal public service 34
A personal distillation of what we learned. 36
The decline of open critical thinking 36
Lack of gumption. 37
Paradoxes, neuroses and willful blindness 38
Conclusion 41
Annex: Basic documentation for each session 44

Chapter 2 Cat's eyes:
the capacity to engage intelligently. 47
A syncretic view of each theme discussed 48
Intelligent accountability 48
Intelligent regulation. 50
Intelligent organizational design. 52
Intelligent public service. 54
A personal distillation of what we learned. 56
A cautionary statement 56

Somebody is in charge and it is not me. 59
Déformation professionnelle 60
Cognitive dissonance. 62
The presence of latent fear 63
Conclusion 65
Annex: Basic documentation for each session 67

Chapter 3   Not in the catbird seat:
the capacity to collibrate 69
A syncretic view of each theme discussed 70
Perverse incentives. 70
Rewarding failure and deception. 71
Punishing success. 73
Positive discrimination 74
Failure to confront 76
Pathologies and challenges. 77
Quantophrenia 77
Performance review 80
Speaking truth to power 81
What role for cities in public governance? 83
A personal distillation of what we learned. 84
Moral vacancy. 84
Crippling epistemologies 87
Risk aversion and fear of experimentation. 89
Conclusion 91
Annex: Basic documentation for each session 95

Chapter 4   The unwisdom of cats:
the capacity to reframe 97
A syncretic view of each theme discussed 98
The political-bureaucratic interface. 98
The federal public service as a nexus
of moral contracts 101
From leadership to stewardship 103
Deputy Minister: then, now and in the future 106
A personal distillation of what we learned. 108
Difficulty in thinking about systems 108
Experts can't learn … 110
A tiny bit of intellectual nonchalance. 111

Conclusion 112
Annex: Basic documentation for each session 114

Conclusion 115
Four layers of capabilities. 117
A syndrome ... tentatively 119
Cosmology-less wayfinding. 122
The way out and forward ... a catwalk 125
Toward a new covenant through a new
    inquiring system. 128
One starting point 134
In summary 137

References 141

| Introduction

"Forget the names, remember the stories."
Charles Handy

Public administration is a complex affair of *ménage à trois*. It pertains to the interactions among elected officials, bureaucrats and citizens in the face of various challenges, ranging from the need to ensure stability in the provision of public goods required by the citizens, to the obligation to improvise and innovate in refurbishing the stewardship of the public household to redesign new frames of reference because the socio-economy is being transformed. There are a lot of subsidiary characters – holy and unholy – carousing around the main actors and pretending to add value to the game. Some perform useful intermediation services; others are agents of distortion and value reducing.

This on-going game, striving to elicit the most effective wayfinding in the face of uncertainty, and in sometimes hostile territory, is too often represented in the crudest of ways by the media as some form of *commedia dell'arte*, or as some solemn organization charts created by political scientists. These sorts of cartoons provide neither a fair representation of the subtle ways in which these groups, their organizations and their institutions think and interact, nor a meaningful explanation of their actions.

In Canada, there have been too few successful attempts to probe the minds of politicians, of bureaucrats or of citizens to really make sense of how they think. Whatever probing there has been has too often been shoddy and ideological: the epigones of one tribe or the other arguing some sort of superiority (and therefore some hegemony) over the other two. Values and rationalities have been merrily postulated for one group or the other, with occasional vindication by questionnaires inviting the most grievous self-promotion. However, there has been little appetite for vindication of these claims. All parties have felt comfortable with whatever presumptions conveniently fit their 'needs' in the particular analysis.

These forays have not cast much light on the sources and causes of the failure to evolve forms of coordination (conventions, norms, rules, organizations and institutions) capable of generating the requisite social learning, resilience and capacity to transform what would seem to be required in the public administration of our modern socio-economics. Yet some of these sources and causes of failure have to do with the poverty of mind of one group or the other.

Meaningful mind-probing cannot be satisfied with some over-simplistic depiction of the mindsets of the three groups: politicians as dummies whose policy decisions are guided by anecdotes; bureaucrats as technical experts blinkered by disciplinary blinders, and yet, at senior levels, claiming to know more about what should be done, and to be more legitimate than elected officials; and self-righteous, poorly informed entitlement-inspired citizens, always demanding more but willing to pay ever less, and complaining bitterly about the incapacity of the other two groups to work together to meet their unreasonable expectations.

It has always been our view that neither such derogatory caricatures nor the opposite celebratory, self-adorning, promotional statements by office-holders produce reliable images of the central actors' mindsets. What are needed are occasions when these different groups can 'reveal' indirectly and unwittingly, through conversations about issues of consequence, their capabilities and incapabilities for the ways and means of dealing with them.

This short book, using such an oblique approach, aims at correcting some of the misapprehensions in good currency related to the bureaucratic mindset of Canadian federal senior executives in the early 21st century.

Our reason to start with this group is simply that we are most familiar with it. One of the authors is a senior career public servant (Ruth Hubbard) who served for more than a decade as deputy minister at the federal level in Canada, and was president of the Public Service Commission of Canada. Since retirement, she has been involved in coaching senior public servants in Ottawa. The second is a senior academic and journalist who has spent a considerable amount of time writing about the federal public service, has received a Citation for Public Service by the Association of Public Executives of the Government of Canada (APEX) for this work, and has been involved in professional development for public sector executives in the last few decades.

This volume draws on the extensive experience of these two individuals, and focusses on the results of their recent opportunity to probe the bureaucratic mind by having extensive conversations about taboo topics with a large number of senior federal executives. This opportunity, afforded by APEX, was to conduct 44 sessions of 'discussions' on 24 different topics, with approximately 100 senior executives of the Canadian federal government. These sessions were held between 2006 and 2009, and provided a unique occasion to update earlier experiences. It also led to a number of interviews conducted afterward with other senior federal executives on the same themes.

Preliminary reports on these conversations have been published in a few papers (Hubbard and Paquet 2010), but we have not yet had the occasion to pull together our full reflections on this material, and present the hypotheses suggested by this limited but significant exploration of the bureaucratic mind – a *travail* that has occupied us over a long period of time.

Given the centrality of the APEX-sponsored sessions as the occasion for our reflections to crystallize, we should be clear about APEX's role in those sessions. APEX's sole responsibility was to provide a safe space where executives could engage in serious conversations on some of the difficult problems that they face. This was an opportunity for what Michael Schrage (2000) would call "serious play" with daunting wicked policy problems: challenging ideas, playing with promising prototypes, or intriguing hypotheses. It was an occasion for the participating senior bureaucrats to reveal how they and their colleagues think.

As *animateurs* of those sessions, the authors were fully and solely responsible for the conduct of the sessions, and the preparation of the synthesis of these discussions, but the participants, on the whole, ran the show.

Beyond the traditional *clichés*

To understand the nature of our inquiry, one must start with an acknowledgement of the two *clichés* in good currency about the bureaucratic mindset: the bureaucrat as a utility-maximizing individual *à la* Niskanen (1971), and the bureaucrat as cleric with a noble calling to serve the public interest (Gow 2008).

The first one represents the public service bureaucrat as an individual like all others, seeking to maximize his own utility by making the highest and best use of all the resources at his disposal (including those available to him from the public household). As such, this person is neither better nor worse than any other citizen, and his/her status as a bureaucrat in the public sector should entail no particular privilege or penalty. He should be rewarded according to performance, and he should be entitled to no special benefits. On the other hand, one should not expect from him any more loyalty than that which is expected from employees in the private or social sectors.

The second one represents the public service bureaucrat as a virtuous person with a calling, whose burden of office is quite different from the usual employee. This bureaucrat is seen as a member of a clergy, owing allegiance first and foremost to the conservation of the democratic state and to justice. This entails that he temper his loyalty to his personal wants, and that he can be expected to receive particular benefits for this loyalty to 'higher values' – a loyalty that would lead him to blow the whistle on actions that are harmful to the state (Gow 2008: 115).

There is a wide array of rationales, gradations and conditions attached to the diverse definitions of the burden of office of this group, and a Jesuitical protocol attached to the adjudication of what is or is not warranted therein. Fundamentally, it is assumed that public sector bureaucrats are not like other employees and deserve a variety of privileges because of the 'higher quality' of their work. This ontological view is held by a significant portion of the public administration tribe (practitioners and academics). Most studies that have claimed to 'demonstrate' this ontological view, through self-reporting questionnaires or the like, or through hagiographical works glorifying the accomplishments of particular saintly individuals in the tribe, have done little beyond persuading those already beholden to this view.

Most senior bureaucrats are neither more exclusively self-centred and myopic than their colleagues in the private and social sectors, as some have argued, nor do they seem to have the saintly attributes, the capacity and wisdom to pose as an omniscient group capable of dealing in a superior way with all the challenges they face. Consequently, there may be reasons to question the special status of public sector bureaucrats as extraordinary employees by definition. Their qualifications need to be better ascertained, their burden of office better specified, their performance better gauged, and whatever special privileges are bestowed on them curtailed to match the reality of their special contributions.

The rise of network governance

Over the last few decades, Canada's institutional order has been going through a major transition. It has evolved slowly from a dominance of Big G (government) – centralized, hierarchical and state-centric – towards a dominance of small g (governance) – decentralized, horizontal, and participative in all of the private, public and social sectors. As explained in Paquet (1999a), this profound change has posed significant challenges for senior public servants in the trenches, as the ground on which they operate was in motion, and the challenges they faced were more daunting.

This transition has entailed:

(1) a diminishing capacity of governments to protect their citizens in a globalized world, subject to accelerated technical and social change;

(2) a need for governments to continually innovate in order to be able to continue to provide citizens, in an effective manner, with the key services they depend on;

(3) a major change in the way public policy and regulation are developed, as it is no longer sufficient to find a policy response that is technically feasible; for it to be likely to succeed, the response must also be socially acceptable, politically not too destabilizing, and capable of rallying the collaboration of all the required partners (Paquet 1999b: chapters 2, 5); and

(4) a need to reform the public service accordingly.

Such public administration reforms command a significant change in both the 'what' and the 'how' of public service work. They rattle the very foundations of the shared belief system, based on the presumptions (1) that the state is capable of distilling and articulating the common will of the citizenry across a broad range of domains; (2) that it is also capable of taking charge of the wayfinding; and (3) that it can ensure a stewardship based on shared values that only the state can distill well. The questions raised about these beliefs have made senior public servants (who have a significant investment in this belief system) quite uncomfortable.

The modern world, plagued with complexity, dilemmas and mixed messages about risk management – one needs to be bold but error is not allowed, etc. – has forced a re-jigging of the whole set of arrangements among the three parties in the governing apparatus. Power, resources and information are widely distributed into many heads and hands, and collaborative governance is required, but tensions persist between the still highly-centralized and top-down governing apparatus that remains in place, and the emerging decentralized, bottom-up governance network, even though the former apparatus proves more and more incapable of delivering what it promises (Martin 2014). It is against this backdrop that the safe spaces sessions were carried out.

Over the last century, the public, the bureaucrats and the elected officials have become much more educated and sophisticated. Their information base and their modes of communication and interaction with one another have also become both richer and more complex, and the intermediation work of the media and other connectors (like lobby groups) has often generated important distortions that have made collaboration a rather daunting task, given the variety of networks within which agents are operating *de facto* a regime of network governance.

The new complexity generated by the transformation of the environment and of the institutional order, on the one hand, and by the consequent need for bureaucrats to adjust their frames of reference if their nudging activities are to be effective, on the other hand, has created quite a challenge: maintaining some sort of adequacy between these evolving realities and the frames of reference in use. It has not always been fully recognized that what we call complexity is often nothing more than a name for a new order calling for a new frame of reference. Consequently, it has not been fully realized that the reluctance to abandon old paradigms, in which so much investment has been made, is often responsible for fundamental learning disabilities.

One main source of these learning disabilities is that, despite the fact that nearly all of our success as organisms in modern times is driven by understanding systems, most of us feel that we do not really need to understand systems to succeed in our ordinary daily lives (Pritchett 2013: 142-143). This has led too many to believe that it is not necessary to understand systems. For bureaucrats, this a toxic mistake: refusing to spend "the requisite time to understand" what the new order looks like, how it works, and what can be done to nudge it in particular ways, because this means having to gain some knowledge of a new and more complex paradigm. This may have been inconsequential in earlier times, but as the transformation has proceeded more fully, the disconnection between the new reality and the old map in use that bureaucrats are clinging to has become consequential.

The federal bureaucracy under siege

Some may bemoan the fact that the federal bureaucracy has not transformed in the right way, and that the bureaucrats have not distilled the requisite new paradigms to gauge this evolving environment and to calibrate their actions, but a dramatic transformation of the basic context has occurred.

First, there has been a growing administrative intermediation that has materialized to coordinate an ever more complex and fractured context. The need to find ways to mobilize and maintain collaboration has generated (and has had to adjust to) a much higher degree of complexity and interdependency to an array of new rules, norms and self-censorships. Fundamentally, this has forced all the potential partners to become spectral, to decompose themselves to adapt and adjust to the different contexts in which they operate. The partners no longer live in an old-style community; they cohabit in networks. And, in order to be able to operate well in this world, they must be able to disconnect at will, without risk, and at any time to switch off certain of the multiple constraints. This has impacted all forms of organizations in the latter half of the 20th century (Guillaume 1999; Goldsmith and Eggers 2004).

Second, being in a switching mode has induced a greater propensity to disconnect and to have limited loyalty to any of those multiple allegiances or commitments to would-be collaborators. When parties break promises, when dissenting voices are unlikely to be listened to, but also when exiting the collaborative arrangement is too costly for a dispirited party, disloyalty kicks in. Disgruntled parties feel trapped within an arrangement and the likelihood of internal sabotage is heightened (Paquet 2010).

Third, these two families of forces were compounded in Canada when the traditional public service culture at the federal level came under attack in the 1990s.

The traditional culture in the Canadian federal public service in the third quarter of the 20th century was largely implicit, yet its principles were clear: appointments were made on merit, with minimal political interference; they were preferably made from within; and assistance to public servants in their career pursuits was assured. In the 1990s, this culture was challenged in two ways: from within by Public Service 2000 (PS 2000), and from without by tough financial realities.

The first challenge (efforts to get the public service to better serve the needs of the citizenry, to be more creative and accountable) was labeled PS 2000, and tilted the mindset towards a more citizen-centred service delivery. It did not shake the traditional culture much despite the brouhaha.

The second challenge came when Program Review (1994-99) reduced the size of the public service by nearly 15 percent, and substantially restructured federal government activities. It was an attack on the public service's traditional culture. The directors of personnel said as much in 1994, by declaring the career public service regime in place as "unrealistic, neither necessary nor affordable." It proposed an alternative: the end of indeterminate employment after five years, and the replacement of the regime in place with one where the employees would have to shoulder full responsibility for career planning, with the employer agreeing only to help maintain continued employability of staff.

This proposal to rescind the traditional culture was not *de facto* adopted, but the very fact that it was discussed sent a clear signal that a new era had begun, and that it was necessary to start reframing the sort of approach one would have to take to the governance of the federal public service (Paquet 2009a: 179ff) – one in which the old moral contract between the state and the bureaucracy would have to be replaced by a new one.

Morale was affected and there was a massive demobilization of the public service.

Although not all the things that went wrong over the last few decades in the governance of the country can legitimately be ascribed to this factor, it is equally most unlikely that none of the difficulties can be ascribed to the failures of senior executives. Senior executives play a pivotal role in the complex interfaces with the elected officials and the public. The fact that they have not done as well as expected in such difficult circumstances may be ascribed to some extent to their crippling epistemologies and to the waning of their *affectio societatis* – i.e., commitment to the common public enterprise. Their lack of critical and creative thinking, their wallowing in surreal self-serving fictions and ineffective administrative processes, and their rampant disloyalty to their political masters are matters for which senior executives must be held accountable (Clark and Swain 2005; Paquet 2009b, 2010). Moreover, to the extent that the bureaucratic mindset is responsible for governance failures, it would appear to be imperative to explore ways in which it might be repaired or upgraded to do a better job – a matter we deal with in the conclusion.

The process

In this inquiry, we are trying to understand the way bureaucrats think, and the sort of governance failures that may be ascribable to the way bureaucrats think. The possibility of gauging it through an examination of the series of discussions with senior federal executives (EXs) emerged only as the series of conversations progressed. The opportunity for launching the series originated from a number of EXs who expressed a degree of frustration with the new and challenging issues that were emerging; a realization that confronting such problems required the development of new skills; and that yet there seemed to be no safe spaces where discussions could be carried out, the required new skills honed, and social learning generated about these matters.

We designed four sets of conversations with them that raised wicked problems.[1] The intent was not to search for a quick fix or a solution, but to look at how executives deal

[1] Problems where the goals are not known or are very ambiguous, means-ends relationships are poorly understood and highly uncertain, and the current society does not have the capacity to resolve them (Rittel and Webber 1973).

with the problems, while at the same time developing some capability for problem definition, for learning, for honing of skills. This tended to reveal learning abilities and disabilities.

To deal with such problems effectively, senior public servants had to learn the configuration of both facts and values 'on the job': learning by doing, learning by deliberating. They had to learn from the stakeholders as well as from the many peripheral groups who are in possession of important local knowledge, and from colleagues and experts. Without the help and participation of this whole range of partners, no meaningful collaborative solution can be usefully elicited and implemented. Such competencies must be learned.

Without meaning to anticipate what these discussions with public service senior executives may or may not reveal about particular lacunae in the sort of competencies required, it has now been well established what new/enhanced competencies have to be developed if the bureaucrats of modern time are to be able to deal effectively with the emerging new order, using a more systemic approach:

(a) contextual competencies (acknowledging uncertainty, embracing error, building bridges and strengthening links, reframing problems to explore new solutions);

(b) interpersonal and enactment skills (consultation, negotiation, facilitation, conflict resolution, capacity to adopt new roles and attitudes);

(c) a capacity to create an effective corporate culture (one of productivity, responsiveness, creativity, and learning); and

(d) a will to invent new ways (abandoning a focus on rights and autonomy, when the actual circumstances of life make imperative the acceptance of obligations, interdependence and experimenting with new tools) (Michael 1980; Paquet 1999b: 37-38).

With respect to the conduct of the APEX series, on each of the topics, background material was circulated in advance to provide some basic information (see the list in the annexes at the end of each chapter). Then one of the authors acted as *animateur,* and set the stage for the discussion with a short introduction of the issue. A general discussion followed around a few tentative hypotheses, but there was no attempt to restrict the conversation to these hypotheses.

The discussions were conducted explicitly under Chatham House rules – nothing said there could be mentioned with attribution to any person. This has led to significantly sanitized notes about these conversations being prepared in order to protect the identity of the participants and also to honour our commitment to discretion about the contents of these conversations. The very carefully worded notes written about each conversation were circulated to participants, and we received no complaints or objections to these summaries from any participant. We took this to mean that no one found the contents of these summaries (that are reproduced in the relevant chapters below) objectionable in any way, as far as we are aware.

As mentioned earlier, in revisiting the material from these sessions for the preparation of this volume, we have taken the opportunity of drawing from subsequent discussions with some of the participants, and some interviews with additional Canadian federal senior public servants to complement and finesse the earlier material.

The outcome: probing a mindset

Exploring the state of mind of senior Canadian federal bureaucrats – an afterthought of this exercise – is a daunting task. Our very limited forays do not aim to provide an in-depth definitive perspective on this complex territory. We have garnered impressions from only a small fraction of this overall group of senior federal government executives. Yet we have had extensive conversations both in class and more informally outside of class with these people, and we heard not only echoes of frustration, but also a lot of information and suggestions about what was perceived as the dynamics at play.

Two dark clouds cast a shadow over all our discussions with senior executives:

(1) a sense of betrayal as a result of the mid-1990s discussions about the federal government's rescinding of the moral contract between the government and its senior bureaucrats (Paquet 2009: chapter 8); even though this pronouncement never got carried into law, it left deep scars;

(2) a growing alienation between politicians and bureaucrats has materialized, and has been felt as a result of the arrival in power of alternative governments whose perspectives were rooted in philosophies and belief systems that have appeared to be in conflict with those of bureaucrats hired, groomed and promoted by earlier governments This, added to the 1990s sense of betrayal, has contributed significantly to the deterioration of the rapport between politicians and bureaucrats. The situation was further poisoned by a constant stirring of the potential for animosity and hostility between the two groups by the media, unsympathetic to the new government, and by zealots of the minority parties and of their academic and bureaucratic colleagues, talking about the impossibility of working with the new so-called autocratic and non-progressive government.

The summaries of the discourse have been sanitized of precise examples and illustrations to preserve the confidentiality of the participants, so they may appear somewhat bland, but the conversations were rich in testimonies that have influenced our conclusions.

Given these atmospherics, we have tried, however imperfectly, in the four chapters that follow to gauge what might be derived from our conversations. In chapter 1, we explore the senior bureaucrats' capacity to cope with evolving contexts, interfaces and organizational features; in chapter 2, we go on to examine their capacity to engage intelligently with the challenges of the new *modus operandi* confronting bureaucrats with more paradoxical situations; chapter 3 focusses on their capacity to collibrate[2] in the face

---

[2] To collibrate is to interfere subtly to compensate for certain biases or untoward situations in the manner one might interfere with the normal working of a scale by way of a finger to correct such an untoward situation.

of perverse incentives and toxic pathologies; and in chapter 4, we discuss their capacity to reframe their perceptions and systems of belief, and to engage in the necessary redesign of organizations when confronted with significant transformation in the basic references defining their work.

The content of these four chapters enables us to probe different layers of the bureaucratic mind as the participants were confronted with gradually more demanding questions. The lessons learned from these different sets of conversations in the series converge somewhat. We have tried in the general conclusion to show this.

This work could not have been done without the open-minded and generous collaboration of APEX. For this help, support and confidence, we are most grateful to Pierre DeBlois and Michel Smith. However, APEX should not in any way be held responsible for whatever inferences we have drawn from these conversations carried out under their auspices nor for the conclusions we have derived from them.

The many-faceted support of the Centre on Governance of the University of Ottawa in this project is also gratefully acknowledged.

For those who might be intrigued by our continuous reference to cats throughout this book, it is meant to remind both the authors and the readers that our efforts to read the bureaucratic mind have had to be oblique and therefore could lead only to tentative conclusions. The world of cats is very complex: Schrödinger's cat is both dead and alive, and, of Lewis Carroll's Cheshire cat, it is said that it can appear and disappear, and that we only see its grin. Similarly, any of our conclusions from this exercise must be hyper-prudent and they must also be read as tentative.

Our cautionary tale should be read with these paradoxes in mind, and not as a catcall – a loud and raucous cry expressing disagreement. This is not a catcall; we are only expressing concern.

References

Clark, Ian and Harry Swain. 2005. "Distinguishing the Real from the Surreal in Management Reform: Suggestions from Beleaguered Administrators in the Government of Canada," *Canadian Public Administration*, 48(4): 453-476.

Goldsmith, Stephen and William D. Eggers. 2004. *Governing by Network*. Washington, DC: Brookings Institution.

Gow, J. Iain. 2008. "Between Ideals and Obedience: A Practical Basis for Public Service Ethics" in *Professionalism and Public Service – Essays in Honour of Kenneth Kernaghan*. David Diegel and Ken Rasmussen (eds.). Toronto, ON: University of Toronto Press, p. 98-126.

Guillaume, Marc. 1999. *L'empire des réseaux*. Paris, FR: Descartes & Cie.

Hubbard, Ruth and Gilles Paquet. 2010. *The Black Hole of Public Administration*. Ottawa, ON: The University of Ottawa Press.

Martin, Roger L. 2014. "The Big Lie of Strategic Planning," *Harvard Business Review*, 92(1-2): 78-84.

Michael, Donald N. 1980. *The new competence: The organization as a learning system*. San Francisco, CA: Values and Lifestyles Program.

Niskanen, William A. 1971. *Bureaucracy, Representative Government and Representation*. Chicago, IL: Aldine.

Paquet, Gilles. 1999a. "Innovations in Governance in Canada," *Optimum*, 29(2-3): 71-81.

Paquet, Gilles. 1999b. *Governance Through Social Learning*. Ottawa, ON: University of Ottawa Press.

Paquet, Gilles. 2009a. *Scheming virtuously: The road to collaborative governance*. Ottawa, ON: Invenire Books.

Paquet, Gilles. 2009b. *Crippling Epistemologies and Governance Failures – A Plea for Experimentalism*. Ottawa, ON: The University of Ottawa Press.

Paquet, Gilles. 2010. "Disloyalty," *www.optimumonline.ca*, 40(1): 23-47.

Pritchett, Lant. 2013. *The Rebirth of Education – Schooling ain't Learning*. Washington, DC: Brookings Institution.

Rittel, H.W.J. and M.M. Webber. 1973. "Dilemmas in a General, Theory of Planning," *Policy Sciences*, 4, p. 155-169.

Schrage, Michael. 2000. *Serious Play*. Boston, MA: Harvard Business School.

| Cat's cradling: the capacity to cope

"No damn cat, and no damn cradle."
Kurt Vonnegut jr.

"Cat's cradle" is the name of a children's game – producing endless designs using fingers and a loop of string. It has been played around the world for hundreds of years, but, in modern times, the expression has been used to connote intricacy and complexity.

Coping is neither problem-solving, nor finding the solution to a puzzle. In these sorts of cases, the issue or problem is relatively well-defined, and the challenge is to find a technical answer to a well-circumscribed problem. Coping refers to situations that are much less well-defined, and where the problem itself is ill-defined. What is involved is not a neat solution to be discovered, but some sort of grappling with a complex, evolving and taxing situation that will only lead to a response. The degree of imprecision and the ill-structured sense of the challenge being faced are the main features of the issue. The information is by definition incomplete, and most often contested. Thus, one is condemned to finding one's way, to groping in the hope of wayfinding by experimentation. This is the way of social learning (Paquet 2012; Paquet 2013).

Coping depends on individual characteristics, but also on the organizational and institutional fabric of the context, and on the more or less stressful nature of the broader environment. Some of these dimensions are constraints that can only be internalized and adapted to; others refer to dimensions that are tractable and can be modified, and draw attention to capacities and competencies that can be developed and perfected to do so – capacities that depend on personal assets, sentiments and temperament (Foa 1971). It is the conjunction of individual, organizational and environmental circumstances, with the degree of toxicity of the situation, that will determine what mechanism will be used to cope.

These mechanisms may range over a wide spectrum to deal with diverse ailments: from cognitive dissonance and denial, to rationalizing submissive adjustment to circumstances, to trivializing by making small something that is really big, to avoiding the issue altogether. The mechanisms may work at changing the way one thinks, at changing one's behaviour, at designing effective ways to reduce harm, etc.[3]

We have not attempted to forcefully fit the Canadian federal executives' reactions to the problems discussed in this chapter into such categories. We have been satisfied to listen to them in order to ascertain how they think, how they seem to react to the problems they were confronted with, and in what ways.

A syncretic view of each theme discussed

For the first phase of our project, we selected two topics in each of the following four different areas: contextual issues (diversity and security), interpersonal rapport (ethics and disloyalty), organizational culture (corporate culture and the Gomery world), and new governance tools (public-private partnerships and a new partitioning of the public service).

Contextual issues and interpersonal rapport

Diversity

Great population movements are rearranging the demographic face of the world. Not only is diversity (linguistic, cultural,

---

[3] For a broader but tractable survey of the sorts of coping mechanisms that are most often mentioned in psychology, see http://changingminds.org/explanations/behaviors/coping/coping.htm.

ethnic, etc.) growing in most countries, but it is also becoming deep diversity, i.e., translating into deep cleavages. Are there limits to diversity? What does that mean for the public service, both on the policy front and for its own fabric and practices?

The notion of diversity is quite complex. It connotes a range of things: from a basic demographic fact, to an ideology about what is desirable, to a plea for 'fraternity lite'. For all sorts of reasons, Canada has been drifting from being a *de facto* polyethnic society to choosing, as a matter of policy, to become a multicultural one. This has generated tensions. In Canada, for the time being, two broad approaches are in good currency: interculturalism in Quebec and multiculturalism in the rest of Canada. *Grosso modo*, the key difference between the two is that, in the former case, many things would appear not to be negotiable, while in the latter case, almost everything would appear to be negotiable under the rubric of reasonable accommodation.

Two key questions were discussed: Are there limits to diversity? Can we negotiate moral contracts among groups as part of citizenship building?

In our conversation, there was a clear consensus that some things are not negotiable: acceptance of Canada's legal framework (the Criminal Code and the Charter of Rights and Freedoms) was seen as a minimum. Beyond this, participants generally agreed that there may be additional non-negotiable items that could only be arrived at through conversation and dialogue (Yankelovich 1999).

Paradoxically, while there was a sense that conversations about such issues are necessary, at the same time there was palpable unease about conducting such discussions. The basic reason was that, while these conversations were clearly seen from a Cartesian point of view as essential if the mutual expectations of the different groups are to be clarified and understood, there was also concern that these conversations might lead to 'either-or' confrontations rather than compromises of the 'more-or-less' variety. The sense was that, at times, political correctness and intimidating fundamentalism might make it difficult, if not impossible, to avoid being led to unreasonable accommodations. It was feared that participants in these conversations would tend to reluctantly accept such unreasonable accommodations at a superficial level to avoid outright conflict that they would profoundly resent in their heart of hearts. This makes the emergence and negotiation of moral contracts (i.e., agreements about mutual expectations) very difficult, and explains the tendency for many to prefer some senseless *laissez-faire* based on the optimistic faith that peaceful coexistence will somehow emerge.

On the other hand, it was readily agreed that moral contracts are negotiated and renegotiated informally throughout the land every day. While this point was generally agreed to, the very notion of moral contracts generated some concern because of it sounding like rules. So the paradoxical conclusion was that the best strategy is perhaps engaging in moral contracting through extensive conversations, but at all costs, to avoid talking about it as contracting.

Three points on which there was a strong consensus were that:

(1) diversity should not be used to obtain special privileges;

(2) more mechanisms are needed to promote dialogue and to clarify mutual expectations; and

(3) priority should be given to eliminating minor irritants, and these minor successes should be used as a way to make easier any discussion about more problematic issues that would make more robust negotiations and accommodations more difficult to swallow.[4]

Security

Most of our daily life is orchestrated by rules (e.g., speed limits on the road, etc.) that have a well-defined, probable mortality

---

[4] The hypersensitivity of such discussions and the great danger of their being hijacked by fundamentalists has been amply illustrated by a very carefully prepared and immensely sensitive and sensible manual to help immigrants better integrate in Gatineau, QC being withdrawn by officials on the basis of a single objection by one immigrant, and by the *débordements* that have been generated by the discussions around the proposed ill-conceived *Charter of Values* in Quebec in the fall of 2013.

rate attached to them. They embody an implicit trade-off between willed security and the fact that some costs may be regarded as unbearable.

On this front, citizens are attracted by the precautionary principle as a guidepost. In its weak form, it requires taking preventative measures in advance, just in case something undesirable might occur; in its strong version, it claims entitlement to 100 percent protection, and rules ensuring that this will be accomplished. Indeed, the radically strong version of the precautionary principle asserts that 100 percent security *must* be provided by the state, and by public servants acting on its behalf, and insists that public servants be clairvoyant: 'you should have known' is the response to an unfortunate event (tainted blood, collapsing bridge, etc.) and 'since you did not protect me 100 percent, I will sue and demand compensation.'

In the language of elementary statistics, the balancing between Type I error (rejecting as false what is in fact true) and Type II error (accepting as true what is in fact false) is the challenge. Responsible citizens agonize over the terrible ordeal of those suffering from Type II error (e.g., Arar's deportation and subsequent imprisonment in Syria) but would certainly never forgive the authorities for not having stopped a home-grown terrorist from perpetrating his/her deed if it were known afterward that there was reasonable suspicion that it might happen (Type I error). Bureaucrats want a balance between these possibilities but are hesitant to confront these issues openly, and to talk about the trade-offs that one can and cannot live with.

Two questions were posed: What if the best we can do is to correct both types of error as quickly as possible, since we are bound to make both types of mistakes? Is Canada too complacent about ensuring security, and therefore more vulnerable to Type I error than it should be, as some suggest?

There was a general agreement that Canada was too complacent about ensuring security, and too reluctant to discuss the Type I/Type II error trade-offs explicitly and openly.

Technically, risk depends on the nature of the threat (intent + capacity), and preventive action depends on a mix of the level of risk + the nature of the consequences + the resources available to avoid them. But from the point of view of the authorities, risk is not only a technical matter: it raises questions about our confidence in our basic institutions.

Debates on these issues often occur behind closed doors, and the discussions may become distorted because they are permeated by both the fear of creating a panic, and of contributing to basic institutions losing their credibility.

The result is that security issues are not discussed as much and as openly as they should be, and the authorities are much more willing to allow terrorists and criminals to remain free (Type I error) than to take the chance of having an innocent person incarcerated (Type II error). The cost of this structural imbalance may be high.

Ethics

People have a very vague notion of ethics. Usually it connotes nothing more than doing the right thing. But what does this mean? Public servants are constantly faced with ethical dilemmas, and there is a whole industry trying to persuade them that there are codes and rules that may hold the mechanical key to ethical behaviour. These devices, like 16th century maps, are usually elegant but not very useful to navigation.

Learning to navigate in order to stay within the 'moral corridor' means taking into account (1) the facts of the situation being faced; (2) an appreciation of the room to manœuvre that is regarded as permissible in a given organization (its culture); and (3) a few fundamental principles that may be held dear. This can only happen through discussing a great number of cases (real or imaginary). But it has to be recognized from the very beginning that no measuring rod can be devised that can reduce ethical dilemmas to technical problems, and make them mechanically 'resolvable' (despite vain attempts by philosophers and others to suggest it can be done).

A useful vocabulary has been proposed by Kolhberg (1981) to help the thinking about moral development. He suggests that there are six stages of increasing moral development. The right action is taken (1) to avoid punishment, (2) to serve one's own needs, (3) so others will view you as a good person, (4) to abide by law and authority, (5) to abide by moral contracts, and (6) as a recognition of principles of justice, fairness and universal rights.

The 'burden of office' of senior public servants requires something more in the way of duties and responsibilities than what is expected of citizens-at-large or business people (i.e., he or she might be required to operate at Kohlberg's level (5), while, for others, it may be permissible or tolerable to operate at level (4)).

Moreover, in today's small g (governance) world – where power, resources and information are distributed among many partners, and collaboration is an imperative – doing the right thing does not only mean meeting the expectations from higher ups (as was the case in the Big G world), but also meeting the expectations of a vast circle of stakeholders and partners (i.e., a kind of 360° degree circle of expectations). Nowadays, moral contracts exist between senior public servants and many other groups – citizens, taxpayers, colleagues, partners in service delivery, etc. – that may tug them in different directions. And these expectations may neither be compatible nor commensurable one with the other. This means that senior public servants must find creative ways to square this circle, and to navigate the moral corridor safely if they are to fulfill their burden of office.

Two questions were discussed: first, is there a decline in the ethics of public servants (i.e., is the senior public service failing more often than before in meeting level (5) standards – abiding by the moral contracts they have agreed to)? And second, are there things that can be done to strengthen the capability of senior public servants to meet this standard, and tools that they can use to enable them to do so?

The ensuing discussion made reference to a variety of pressures on senior public servants that may drive them to stay at level (4) – abiding by law and authority. The multiplication of rules, the lack of safe spaces for dialogue, and the relative lack of support from higher up on this front have caused a chill and a good deal of risk aversion. It was also strongly felt that the great amount of talk about ethics these days might only mask a reduction of trust. If there is no trust, working in partnerships becomes more difficult and takes more time. Learning is not easy; and it is harder to have the discussions necessary to help public servants develop the tools they need to get better at navigating the moral corridor safely and living up to their burden of office.

There was a sense that the flexibility required to be allowed to try to do the right thing, by fully exploring what is really possible within the spirit of the law, needed to be regained.

In the meantime, several ideas emerged as potential avenues that could be pursued to improve the present situation:

(1) taking on more risk personally and for the team ("I will back you having a bit more room to manoeuvre");

(2) accepting mistakes as necessary for learning (even rewarding well-executed failures);

(3) talking things through with the team and others, both beforehand and afterwards;

(4) asking and accepting "what is reasonable in the circumstances?" i.e., operating within the spirit as well as the letter of the law;

(5) stopping the cycle of mistrust (e.g., opening the books of an operation to a partner who is mistrustful, and not expecting reciprocal action until some trust has been built up);

(6) giving people the opportunity to speak up about their frustrations; and

(7) using one's influence to try to push the envelope a little with bosses or with the system.

To enable public servants to navigate the moral corridor safely in today's difficult climate, it was felt that, first, it had to be framed as calling for moral imagination to be used (scheming virtuously), to live up to the expectations of the different moral contracts of stakeholders; and second, the capacity and possibility of learning from individual cases had to be made possible by senior managers acting as enablers.

Disloyalty

Disloyalty was a most difficult topic to deal with because it cut closer to the bone. It involved – of necessity – emotions and a sense of self-incrimination. Every public servant feels loyal, and is quite good at rationalizing this conviction. Yet, in reality, the public servants' burden of office is built on many unwritten, even un-stated clauses, defining the understandings and expectations of others – bosses, peers, co-workers, clients, possibly subordinates and/or partners – with whom they collaborate. And these may be incompatible one with another.

Disloyalty is breaking any such moral contract deliberately and knowingly.

A particularly difficult series of problems arises for public servants' burden of office when they are expected to shift their loyalty to the new agenda and policies of a new government. When one party has held power for 10 or 15 years, it would be surprising if the old ways had not come to be regarded as normal and preferred. Faced with having to forge new direct and indirect relationships that will call for the acceptance of very different perspectives with which they may not be naturally in accord, public servants have two choices – leaving ('exiting' physically or hibernating by leaving their souls at home) or trying to propose modifications ('voice' alternative views and propose modifications). Whichever road is travelled, some have suggested that a measure of loyalty to the organization/institution may be how long 'voice' is used before 'exiting'. This is a bit simplistic. Openly disagreeing or dissenting is not necessarily a form of disloyalty. On the other hand, passive deceit (e.g., silence, reluctance to raise questions, tardiness in questioning when questioning is warranted) might be clearly disloyal.

The questions raised were: What is disloyalty for senior public servants? Is disloyalty increasing? What concrete actions are called for, if any?

There was much unease among the participants at the very idea of admitting that there is any such a thing as disloyalty in the upper ranks of the federal public service. This unease was attenuated somewhat as the conversation progressed, but never really disappeared. Indeed, a vibrant denial that any such thing exists kept popping up.

It was, in part, a manifestation of the classic tension felt by public officials between 'duty to the public' (as they themselves define it) and 'duty to the higher-ups and partners' in the particular world in which they operate. The question squarely put at the centre of the discussion is "Who should define the public interest: the elected government or the unelected public servants who believe that they know more and claim to know what is best?"

Examples were cited involving the highest levels of the bureaucracy: the behaviour of one deputy minister who chose to leave because he was unable/unwilling to support the new government's approach, while another chose, instead, to "put words in the mouth of his unsuspecting minister." Participants agreed that the first was acting with integrity, while the second was being disloyal.

There was some reluctant agreement that disloyalty had increased recently. It was seen, in part, as a consequence of the increased complexity of the policy issues. Complex issues lend themselves to a multiplicity of interpretations and feed a greater possibility of differences of opinion. For example, blaming an evaluator for not having spoken up loud enough, or scientists for not being clairvoyant enough about future problems may be unreasonable, and may be wrongly associated with disloyalty.

Several participants observed that restoring profession-alism and professional pride might play an important part in restoring loyalty. This might entail taking a leaf from the book of professional associations, which instil pride (e.g., through an oath of office ceremony, continuing education, accreditation) and monitor quality (e.g., disciplinary committees). The new requirements to publish information about wrongdoing were also seen as potentially helpful.

Yet, despite individual dedication and effort, it was reluctantly felt that there seems to be a growing culture of disloyalty enveloping the public service today. It would appear, however, that it is more a 'passive' disloyalty (e.g., responding to the narrowest interpretation of what is expected and required and, as result, reducing the notion of burden of office to something much less than it should be) rather than 'active' disloyalty (e.g., deliberately undermining the work of superiors and/or betraying the trust of partners and citizens).

Organizational culture and new governance tools

Corporate culture

The concept of culture connotes the ideas, customs and skills of a people or a group that are passed along from one generation to the next in some fashion, as well as shared beliefs, behaviours and systems of meanings. In general, the culture of any organization is an appreciative system that is both enabling and limiting. It echoes a set of readiness and capacities, as well as a set of constraints under which the organization labours whenever it faces unforeseen challenges. Corporate culture makes sense of what is, of what actually exists, and of what is important. It helps to create names, interpretations and commitments. It creates a framework for interpretation and understanding.

In fact, the contrasts among corporate cultures become more visible when organizations face an unforeseen crisis for which there is no routine response, and for which the organizations are technically ill-prepared. In these circumstances, the 'soul' and 'instinctive dimensions' of the organization take charge of problem definition and shape the response; these responses reveal the logic of the underlying culture.

Many schemes have been proposed to X-ray corporate culture. One interesting one (for comparative purposes) has been proposed by Geert Hofstede (www.geert-hofstede.com). It focuses on indices of power inequality, individualism, risk aversion and long-term orientation (among other things). On that scale, Canada and Latin American countries are much more risk-averse than the US, and less likely to accept change readily.

This has had an impact on the corporate culture of Canadian organizations in all sectors. As Wahl (2006) reported, we know that only about 36 percent of Canadian executives regard their organizations as having strong adaptive cultures; some 55 percent define their corporate culture as weak (i.e., plagued with top-down managerial arrogance, fear of risk-taking, inward focus, and bureaucracy); 64 percent say that corporate culture is important, and 72 percent say that their organization's culture is not what they desire for the future. Yet nobody appears to know what could be done about it and how.

The questions posed were: Should we be worried about corporate culture? What can we do to influence it?

Participants felt there were good reasons to worry. Most agreed that the current environment for the public service is one of "zero tolerance for error + no risk allowed + political expectations must be met," with a drift towards a culture of blaming rather than accepting that making mistakes is a part of learning. Public sector culture is embedded in a societal culture that is risk averse, so the public service has become risk averse.

Many participants thought that any improvement had to start from above: the fish rots from the head. The deputy ministers should be willing to say "take a risk and we will back you up." The culture would be affected significantly if the Clerk of the Privy Council sent the right signals through his actions: e.g., promoting to the rank of deputy minister people who are courageous. But others believed that this is asking too much, and that the focus should be put instead on asking "What can we do ourselves?"

So at the end of the day, it was felt that a more promising strategy would be bottom up: better to help young managers learn how to confront squarely and explicitly such problems of risk-taking, rather than to avoid taking risks at all costs, as they are often tempted to do. Over time, these bottom-up efforts are likely to change the culture.

The Gomery world

The 1995 referendum on Quebec separation from Canada was held as the result of a *malaise* among a plurality of Quebeckers about the existing institutional order, and about the ways in which the federation was run. On the occasion of the referendum, a substantial number of Quebeckers expressed dissatisfaction with an overly centralized federal system that did not allow Quebec to exercise the full range of public powers needed to ensure its maintenance and progress as a distinct society.

The Gomery Inquiry was triggered by a report from the Office of the Auditor General of Canada about irregularities in the administration of federal sponsorship activities in Quebec between 1996 and 1999. These activities had blossomed in Quebec following the narrow victory of the federalist forces in the 1995 referendum on Quebec secession. Sponsorship activities were intended to increase the visibility and support of the federal government in Quebec, thereby celebrating the benefits of federalism.

Justice John H. Gomery was given a broad mandate: "to investigate and report on questions raised 'directly and indirectly' by the audit." Given the broad Gomery mandate, one might reasonably have expected that this inquiry would not focus narrowly on possible administrative misappropriation of some federal funds for sponsoring publicity events, but would also examine the 'sources' of the unease that had led the Canadian federal government to use these kinds of social marketing activities. The perceived inadequacies of the existing federal system were obviously questions raised 'indirectly' but sharply by the sponsorship affair.

The Inquiry resulted in the publication of two reports – one in the fall of 2005, and the other in the winter of 2006. The reports chose to focus exclusively on the dirty tricks of money laundering, and on how to prevent such incidents in the future by adding many additional sets of administrative controls. They paid no attention to the deeper causes and sources of the problem: the dysfunctions of an existing centralized governing apparatus that is tearing the fabric of the country apart; and the collusion of centralizing groups to defend the *status quo*.

Two questions were tabled: Is the system of Canadian federalism unduly centralized? Does the existing model of Canadian public administration in place today perform as well as is claimed?

Participants generally felt that the current systems of federalism and of public administration were far from perfect, especially in light of the drift underway from Big G (government) toward a small g (governance) world in which no one is fully 'in charge' anymore.

On the issue of federalism and the federal role, participants noted that the federal government was downloading responsibilities and cutting (or increasing) transfers to the provinces in a whimsical way. It was felt that there was a need for some overhauling of fiscal federalism to deal with the current vertical fiscal imbalance (federal/provincial/municipal).

On the issue of public administration: some suggested that the problems were mainly ascribable to 'political' interference, while others felt that "some public servants may be too anxious to please and thus end up becoming too attached to the government of the day." There was some mention of the fact that deputy heads are moved around so quickly that departments/ agencies are often left rudderless for quite some time.

This provoked a conversation about the vulnerability of a system that is built around specific 'leaders' when what Canadians assume is needed (and what is required) is 'system trust': trust that, despite individual failings, the entire system catches mistakes or missteps very quickly and corrects them fast. This is regarded as the basis of effective governance.

Most participants concluded that experimentalism and 'open source federalism' might well provide an avenue for greater effectiveness, with the federal government acting more as 'coach' than a player itself in many issue domains.

With respect to the second question – is the Canadian public administration model as good as claimed – a good deal of defensiveness was evident. Whether this arose as a result of sheer corporatism or as a lack of interest in and/or appreciation of the broader contours of the 'public administration machine' was not clear. Participants seemed keenly aware of the complex arrangements in their own issue domains, but the contours of the broader administrative apparatus appeared to remain not fully understood by many of them. This was somewhat surprising for executive-level public servants.

It is not unfair to add that the conversations revealed a profound attachment to state-centricity, and an equally strong commitment to the 'need' for a strong federal government (and consequently a powerful and influential senior federal public service). References were made to the need for strengthening the role of the federal government, to government being essential to articulate the public interest, and to the state, in our complex world, being the 'sole actor', having the cognitive power and muscle necessary to identify the public good and effectively pursue it. As a result, participants were quite reluctant to chastise the federal government for its centralized mindset or its state centricity. Indeed, it was felt that its final role as arbiter in most files was essential. This should not be surprising from executive-level career federal public servants.

So while experimentalism and open-source federalism as 'general ideas' were received favourably, when it came to making these ideas operational through a robust departure *de facto* from state centricity and from hegemonic overall federal controls, the support for these bold ideas almost disappeared. Consequently, one had a sense that, despite conceding that the Canadian model of public administration was far from perfect, the participants were at best willing to entertain some redecoration of the public household, but not any major architectural repairs.

This state of mind would appear to echo the substance of a lecture of Jocelyne Bourgon (2007):

(1) a recognition, as a result of some factual evidence, but at the most general discursive level, that public administration is a work in progress and requires serious overhauling in Canada and elsewhere; but

(2) an equally strong feeling that there is no need to question the fundamental underlying assumptions on which the traditional model is based.

This allows bureaucrats to escape from the old Hegelian mental prison that makes the state the sole source of the 'common will' (an assumption that is now openly challenged), but also to re-invent the state (in this case with the federal government in the lead) in the form of a quasi-Hegelian intermediary institution that can do almost the same thing in the name of effective provision of public services to the citizenry because it has the unique capacity to read the collective mind appropriately and to serve the citizens well. The 'state' is used here as a code word for bureaucrats.

Public-private partnerships

Everyone agrees that there may be things that one particular sort of arrangement (private, voluntary or public) does better than the others. Equally, there may be some things done best by combining forces across sectors. In recent decades, public-private partnerships (PPPs or P3s) have become popular with reform-minded (and cash-strapped) governments – reducing administrative and operating costs by some 20-50 percent in some areas. Yet there have been also some spectacular P3 failures because the 'winning conditions' were not in place. Moreover, a strong ideological opposition to P3s still prevails in certain public sector circles and is epitomized by Jane Jacobs (1992) who argued that such things can only produce "monstrous hybrids."

There is a poor understanding of the whole panoply of 'winning conditions' necessary for P3s to succeed: engaging the mega-community effectively and continually, ensuring that there is value adding and a fair sharing of the benefits and risks among partners, well-designed contractual arrangements and procedures, and social learning that ensures that the arrangements can be adapted continually to new circumstances.

The questions posed were: Has the case for P3s been made persuasively? What are the winning conditions for successful P3s?

Participants quickly agreed that the case for P3s had been easily made in the case of physical assets (e.g., bridge, road or building construction) – where a clear contract could be written, and where there is a strong element of predictability about the outcome. But they pointed out that the case has not yet been made persuasively about the use of P3s in the delivery of social services. When probed as to why it might not work there, the responses were vague and woolly.

Participants felt that using small steps, and proceeding gradually, would be the best approach to the successful implementation of P3s. A number of successful experiments seem to have been conducted piecemeal, slowly, experimentally, and 'under the radar screen'. Experiments have the advantage that, when they are shown to be successful, they can be generalized more readily, and will gain popular support. It was also suggested that the focus at the beginning might usefully be on experiments outside 'core areas'; for example in health care, P3s might be used in sub-areas where people are in significant pain or discomfort, but where the problem is not life threatening (e.g., joint replacements and cataracts).

Much was made of the need for the public sector to develop the required competencies to negotiate and govern P3s effectively. Such competencies are scattered around many departments and may not be easily mobilized by a single agency. This may be the Achilles' heel of the P3 process.

Possibly more important, and often unnoticed, is a major ideological blockage about P3s in social services areas: P3s might not ensure equal access for the very poor or disadvantaged as a pure public agency would! A discussion followed about the dark side of egalitarianism: "if I can't have it, then neither should you" is making envy into a national virtue, and the emergence of the new norm of 'equability' (i.e., a willingness to eliminate unacceptable inequities only) to replace the old norm of radical egalitarianism (Kekes 2003).

The three main challenges would appear to be (1) a profound distrust of the private sector in Canada; (2) a difficulty for the public sector to mobilize the high-level competencies needed to govern the P3 process effectively; and (3) some deep-rooted commitment to egalitarianism in the Canadian psyche, and a sense that P3 is and must be anti-egalitarian. These stand in the way of a greater use of P3s.

Partitioning anew the federal public service

An important myth in good currency suggests that one of the reasons why state employment cannot be reduced without generating an impoverishment of governance is that 'all' work done in the public sector is, by definition, both:

(1) homogeneous, i.e., by definition 'special' whatever the level and the type of work involved, and

(2) of a different kind – of a 'higher order' than other work – i.e., there can be no substitution of 'lower order work' (private or social sector types) for 'higher order' public sector employment.

In a world that puts a premium on flexibility and innovation, such rigidity cannot easily be defended. A case can be made that public sector employment is neither as different in kind nor as homogeneous as has been presumed – at least not everywhere. So, partitioning public service employment in line with their differential burden of office – with quite different human resource regimes for each grouping – would tend to increase flexibility, effectiveness and efficiency.

Federal public servants could be partitioned in the following way:

I Super-bureaucrats (e.g., the Auditor General and agents of Parliament, deputy ministers and the like: approximately 500 individuals) whose burden of office is co-governing with the elected officials and safeguarding the fabric of society;

II Guardians (e.g., the executives and persons of that sort: approximately 10,000) whose main job is senior management of the public household to ensure optimal productivity;

III Professionals (e.g., scientists, lawyers and the like: approximately 40,000) whose main job is to ensure reliable regulation, innovation and horizontal coordination; and

IV Employees (e.g., approximately 185,000) whose main function is to ensure service delivery with a modicum of reliability and fairness.

The questions raised with the participants were: Is the 'one lump of labour' myth to refer to the federal public service as homogeneous and fundamentally different still alive? What sort of partitioning of public employment might be workable?

Participants generally felt that, despite the existence of different unions (e.g., Public Service Alliance of Canada (PSAC) and Professional Institute of the Public Service of Canada (PIPSC)) with different approaches, the notion of 'one lump of labour' is still in place, and it is an important impediment to getting work done in an environment in which there is a need for a great variety of organizational arrangements.

Tackling the professional grouping (i.e., III) first seemed an attractive idea for there is a sense of communities there. But starting with grouping II (primarily EXs) might be easier. Another way to approach the problem might be to introduce the partitioning in one small organization as an experiment. The concept, if successful, might then be generalized. Unions might be prepared to tradeoff some things (e.g., higher barriers to entry and exit in group IV) in return for being able to bargain new elements (e.g., classification and promotion). Regional rates of pay were also felt to be important. For any such re-partitioning to be successful, it would be crucial to demonstrate that different human resource regimes provide better results for the organization of work and for the welfare of the workers, but also for the general performance of the public workforce.

One would also need to initiate discussion with a view to modifying not only the human resources regimes but also the underlying frame of reference – from the current one that emphasizes accountability almost exclusively (doing only what one has been mandated to do) to one that puts the focus back on the organizational goals of efficiency and effectiveness, and explicitly links the human resources regimes to broad organizational goals and high performance.

A personal distillation of what we learned

The intent of this section is neither to second guess the perspectives of the public sector executives we conversed with nor to psychoanalyze them on the basis of these few conversations. Rather our intent is to draw some more general conclusions about the challenges facing the Canadian public sector on the basis of what these conversations have revealed to us.

The decline of open critical thinking

First, it became clear over those months of conversations that there is a lack of safe spaces where executives are allowed and enabled to explore these thorny issues – where there is no precise or definitive solution but only responses with varying degrees of usefulness. Safe space discussions were celebrated as automatically generating a degree of critical thinking, some recognition that organizations have failed, and an appreciation of what might have been done better. A sense developed during our conversations that this kind of forum is not being universally welcomed precisely because it might generate critical thinking. The shadow of yesteryears, under the realm of a certain Clerk of the Privy Council for whom criticism was considered as a form of treason, was still ever present.

While the taste and the need for such safe spaces was felt very strongly by the executives we met, and the usefulness of such exercises in critical thinking was much celebrated, it was clear that a great majority of executives have chosen to avoid them completely. A certain demoralization of a large segment of the executive group has led many to withdraw into the 'technical' aspects of their work, to 'hibernate' as some called it – seeing no merit in engaging in discussions that can only get them into trouble.

We were told repeatedly that the general quality of intra-public-service conversations seems to have declined, in part also as a result of a very high degree of political correctness that has come to prevail over the years. The 'real' conversations are more likely to be carried out in the washroom than in the boardroom. Indeed, many participants remarked on the higher degree of self-censorship that has led to a much less effective degree of social learning than is desirable.

Political correctness may not be an adequate label for a syndrome of denial, timidity, failure to confront difficult issues, risk aversion and a sense of helplessness. Lack of engagement, weakness of will and lack of gumption may be more adequate labels.

Lack of gumption

What emerged from our conversations with those claiming to value immensely an opportunity to critically examine the different questions facing senior executives is that, when provided with an opportunity to do so in a safe space, they did not choose to do so with gumption. There was much tiptoeing before they ventured in and some glibness as soon as we got away from generalities.

First, this seemed to be the result of years of self-restraint and self-censorship that has become second nature. Second, it would appear that participants did not feel comfortable entering into the world of systems analysis – below vague generalities but above operational details – i.e., the locus of social architecture and engineering. This was the locus of maximum hesitation to engage in critical thinking. Thirdly, one could not avoid the impression that the reason this arena was so poor in terms of exchange and imaginative contribution was a combination of lack of interest, lack of preparation, and a sense that they had little in the way of understanding of how thinking aloud at this level might ever end up leading to operational improvements – a sense that it was not part of their burden of office to bother about these aspects of governance.

In a way, it was an echo of the learning disability mentioned in the introduction – the false belief that one does not need to understand systems (Pritchett 2013) – and a lack of appreciation for the centrality of organizational design in modern governance (Boland and Collopy 2004) – a matter that will prove extremely damaging as one moves to more and more daunting challenges for senior executives, and on which we return in chapter 4.

The diffidence to indulging in critical thinking and the lack of gumption might explain some paradoxical reactions to the discussions about certain topics like corporate culture, the 'Gomery world' and disloyalty.

Paradoxes, neuroses and willful blindness

While most participants agreed that these 'realities' were an important source of malaise, there was also, at the same time, even in our safe space, a palpable reluctance to engage fully in discussions about their toxic effects. For instance, there was quite a hostile reaction to the results of an exercise (suggested by Kets de Vries 2001) designed to identify the dominant type of neuroses present in different federal public sector organizations. The very use of the word 'neurosis' was clearly perceived as a loaded term (that was seen as implying some kind of disease or unhealthiness), and as a result provoked strong cognitive dissonance and sharp denial.

Yet, in fact, most institutions are more or less neurotic, and Kets de Vries (2001) has simply proposed a typology of neurotic styles plaguing organizations (the characteristics, fantasies, culture and dangers attached to these different styles, and limiting considerably the possibility of critical thinking). They are spelled out in the table below.[5] A cursory

[5] These ideal-types are vignettes that are not necessarily meant to represent realistic pictures of organizations. At best it indicates a prevalent syndrome in a world where real organizations are often a mix of many types. In May 1990, at a management conference held by Statistics Canada at Mont St. Marie, Gilles Paquet used this template to show that Statistics Canada corresponded to the ideal-type for compulsive organizations. This generated much chagrin at the executive level, and resulted in his being shunned by the organization thereafter. So the instrument should be used with care. Kets de Vries has designed a simple questionnaire to determine to what neurotic style one's own organization belongs, and to what extent one fits well within it. In many exercises (with such a questionnaire) in executive development seminars, some variety of diagnoses has often materialized about the nature of the same organization (depending on the points of view of the different actors) but most often there has been a great deal of convergence of diagnoses.

reading of the table will convey a sense of what each sort of iron cage may entail for those operating within such types of organizations. In each case, different ways have to be designed for the neurotic style to be effectively attenuated. Where a dominant neurotic style or another prevails, the design problem poses quite different challenges.

What was surprising was the vibrant hostility toward even envisaging that such mental prisons might be thinkable for federal public organizations, or that they might be detected through some reflections on one's own practice. Denial and willful blindness were flagrant. One would probably record as much denial in the face of any effort to present evidence that would appear to counter individual beliefs than would appear to be generated by the neurotic styles of the organization.

A similar denial syndrome plagued the discussion about the Gomery world: acceptance of a need to change in general (given the difficulties encountered by the federal state), but unwillingness to accept that there cannot be change without changing some of the basic assumptions on which Big G (government) is built. There would appear to be a profound unease about questioning the fundamental assumptions of state centricity and centralization.

The same sort of difficulties arose in the session on disloyalty. Participants volunteered numerous examples of blatant disloyalty, but were in denial generally about the existence of a culture of disloyalty. There were a number of instances when reference to behaviour that might be construed as 'disloyal' was explained as loyalty to the higher purpose of the public interest.

In many of these cases, there seemed to be a visceral need to defend questionable practices on the basis of superior motives – which is not unusual (Brewer et al. 2000) – and a supposedly keener appreciation of the 'Canadian' values on the part of federal public servants. In this latter case, it would appear that the 'myth of Canadian values' as the basis for federal paramouncy is still alive and well in the higher echelons of the Canadian federal public service despite it being quite problematic (Heath 2003).

SUMMARY OF THE NEUROTIC STYLES

	Paranoid (suspicious)	Compulsive	Dramatic	Depressive	Schizoid (detached)
Characteristics	mistrust much info processing hypersensitivity perceived threats centralized power	perfectionism rigid formal code focus on trivia ritualized evaluation dogmatism	self-dramatization overcentralized narcissism 2nd-tier lacking influence exploitativeness	sense of guilt ritualism helplessness unflexibility bureaucracy	non-involvement internal focus estrangement self-imposed barriers to information insufficient scanning of environment
Fantasy	I cannot really trust anybody; I had better be on my guard	I don't want to be at the mercy of events I must control all things	I want to get attention from and impress people	It is hopeless to change the course of events in my offer I am not good enough	The world of reality does not offer any satisfaction so it is safer to remain distant
Culture	fear of attack intimidation uniformity reactive conservative secretive	rigidity inward directed tightly focused obsessive non-adaptive exhaustive evaluation	idealizing hyperactive impulsive bold ventures non participative action for action's sake	lacking initiative decidophobia lacking vigilance leadership vacuum no sense of direction lacking motivation	insecurity conflict ridden indecisive inconsistent narrow perspectives lacking warmth
Dangers	distorsion of reality defensive attitude	fear of making mistakes excessive reliance on rules	overreaction to minor events actions based on appearances	inhibition of action indecisiveness overly pessimistic	bewilderment and aggressiveness emotional isolation

Source: Adapted from Kets de Vries and F.R. Manfred (2001), p. 146-147.

The concern with ethics and moral contracts generated an extremely high level of interest. These issues are of very personal (as opposed to organizational or institutional) interest and participants felt freer to express their sense of frustration as individuals. The use of the notion of a 'moral corridor' to provide a framework for talking about ethical issues, and the use of moral contracts as instruments to frame moral choices were embraced. It is as if one could openly talk about 'personal dilemmas' but one could not entertain as permissible to indict the organization (culture, disloyalty). Indeed, the discussion about the extent to which the Gomery Commission may not have delved as fully and professionally as it should have in exposing as fully as it should have the knowledge that senior Privy Council Office personnel had about the sponsorship activities in Quebec, and about the way in which these super-bureaucrats had conducted themselves, led to a dead silence. One felt that the discussion had stumbled into *lèse-majesté* territory, and that the conversation had entered hyper-taboo land. A vibrant sense of the solidarity of the tribe kicked in (Hubbard and Paquet 2007: 48).

On issues of a more instrumental nature (PPP and public service partitioning), the safe space may not have been necessary. Those topics were discussed openly and clinically. They were regarded as managerial issues that lent themselves to critical analysis. Interestingly, the undertones of ideology (*à la* Jane Jacobs) that were felt constantly during the discussions of touchier issues did not seem to be sufficient to prevent hard-nosed debates and useful conclusions on which most participants could agree.

Conclusion

This experience with conversations on wicked problems (and the follow-up conversations we have had with some participants) has reinforced some of our presumptions: safe space discussions foster more rapid and better prototyping, and enhance learning about the 'what' and the 'how' of changing public service work. They break old moulds and open new vistas. But most importantly, such conversations perform many cleansing functions: (1) they reveal assumptions people are not aware they are making and challenge them; (2) they kill or at least expose and wound bad ideas; and (3) they create a taste for more experimentation and adaptation, for exploration, for more prototyping and more serious play.

Critical thinking generated by intelligent conversations also fed speculation and exploration about the sorts of institutional repairs that are needed for the governance process to meet the new challenges. Critical thinking reveals the weaknesses of the existing institutional order: here are the gaps, what information, what forums and what permissions are missing so that the requisite amount of consultation, negotiation, collaboration and experimentation are allowed to emerge? A supply of new ideas ensues.

But it cannot be denied that there was much reluctance for a large number of EXs to enter this danger zone of critical thinking: it would appear that, in principle, this is a terrain that the best of our group of senior executives were keen to enter, but, in practice, most became somewhat anxious when the time came to participate in this danger zone. It is not surprising. Groups are prone to suppress evidence that runs counter to their basic premises, and holding the same set of pre-suppositions allows members of a group to confirm each other's interpretation of evidence (O'Toole 1995: 168). Critical deliberation may bring down these defence mechanisms.

It is possible that the calling into question the fundamental belief system caused by the drift from Big G (government) to small g (governance) has called for too much of a reframing to be accepted lightly. This might explain the differences in the nature of the conversations when it dealt with 'technical and somewhat peripheral' management issues as opposed to when it dealt with issues that raised 'fundamental' questions about governance – where paradoxes and denials serve routinely to immunize the hard core of assumptions one is not allowed to challenge.

References

Boland, Richard J. and Fred Collopy (eds.). 2004. *Managing by Design*. Stanford, CA: Stanford University Press.

Bourgon, Jocelyne. 2007. "Responsive, Responsible and Respected Government: Towards a New Public Administration Theory," *International Review of Public Administration*, 73(1): 7-26.

Brewer, Gene A. et al. 2000. "Individual Conceptions of Public Service Motivation," *Public Administration Review*, 60(3): 254-264.

Foa, Uriel G. 1971. "Interpersonal and Economic Resources," *Science*, 3969, p. 345-351.

Heath, Joseph. 2003. *The Myth of Shared Values in Canada*. Ottawa, ON: Canadian Centre for Management Development.

Hubbard, Ruth and Gilles Paquet. 2007. *Gomery's Blinders and Canadian Federalism*. Ottawa, ON: The University of Ottawa Press.

Jacobs, Jane. 1992. *Systems of Survival*. New York, NY: Vintage Books.

Kekes, John. 2003. *The Illusions of Egalitarianism*. Ithaca, NY: Cornell University Press.

Kets de Vries, Manfred F.R. 2001. *The Leadership Mystique*. London, UK/New York, NY: Financial Times/ Prentice Hall.

Kohlberg, Lawrence. 1981. *The Philosophy of Moral Development*. New York, NY: Harper & Row.

O'Toole, James. 1995. *Leading Change*. San Francisco, CA: Jossey-Bass.

Paquet, Gilles. 1990. *"The Statistical Agency as Janus,"* mimeo 8p.

Paquet, Gilles. 2012. "La gouvernance, science de l'imprécis," *Organisations & Territoires*, 21(3) : 5-17.

Paquet, Gilles. 2013. "Wicked Policy Problems and Social Learning," *www.optimumonline.ca*, 43(3): 19-34.

Pritchett, Lant. 2013. *The Rebirth of Education – Schooling ain't Learning*. Washington, DC: Brookings Institution.

Wahl, Andrew. 2006. "Culture Shock: A survey of Canadian executives reveals that corporate culture is in need of improvement," *Canadian Business*, June 6.

Yankelovich, Daniel. 1999. *The Magic of Dialogue – Transforming Conflict into Cooperation*. New York, NY: Simon & Schuster.

Annex : Basic documentation for each session

Diversity

G. Paquet & P. Reed. 2003. "Are There Limits to Diversity?" *www.optimumonline.ca*, 33(1): 13-19.

R. Higham. 2005. "Governance of Diversity: What mechanisms?" *www.optimumonline.ca*, 35(4): 60-67.

G. Paquet. 2006. "APEX 2006 Two-Tracked Symposium: A curmudgeon's commentary," *www.optimumonline.ca*, 36(2): 54-62.

R. Higham. 2006. "The passport of convenience phenomenon," *www.optimumonline.ca*, 36(3): 8-11.

G. Paquet. 2006. "Moral contract as enabling mechanism," *www.optimumonline.ca*, 36(3): 12-21.

Security

WIKIPEDIA: Security, Precautionary principle, Type I and Type II Errors

M. Ignatieff. 2004. *The Lesser Evil – Political Ethics in an Age of Terror*. New York, NY: Penguin.

P. Bruckner. 2006. *La tyrannie de la pénitence*. Paris, FR: Grasset.

C.R. Sunstein. 2005. *Laws of Fear – Beyond the Precautionary Principle*. Cambridge, UK: Cambridge University Press.

Ethics

P. Lecours and G. Paquet. 2006. "Communication and Ethics: How to Scheme Virtuously," *www.optimumonline.ca*, 36(2): 12-26.

Disloyalty

A.O. Hirschman. 1970. *Exit, Voice and Loyalty.* Cambridge, MA: Harvard University Press.

Google: exit + voice + loyalty, for examples of the use of this framework

Corporate culture

A. Wahl. 2006. "Culture Shock: A Survey of Canadian executives reveals that corporate culture is in need of improvement," *Canadian Business,* 10(23).

G. Paquet. 2006. "Corporate Culture and Governance: Canada in the Americas" in P. Imbert (ed.). *Converging Dissensus, Cultural Transformations, and Corporate Cultures.* Ottawa, ON: Research Chair in Social and Cultural Challenges in a Knowledge-Based Society, p. 79-115 (available also on www.gouvernance.ca under Publications).

The Gomery world

R. Hubbard and G. Paquet. 2007. *Gomery's Blinders and Canadian Federalism.* Ottawa, ON: The University of Ottawa Press.

J.G. Stein, M. Gibbins and A. Maioni. 2006. *Canada by Picasso: The Faces of Federalism.* Ottawa, ON: Conference Board of Canada.

Public-private partnerships

R. Hubbard and G. Paquet. 2007. "Public-Private Partnerships and the 'porcupine' problem" in G.B. Doern (ed.). *How Ottawa Spends 2007.* Montreal, QC/Kingston, ON: McGill-Queen's University Press.

B. Aubert and M. Patry. 2005. "Les partenariats public-privé : le long et tortueux chemin du Québec, " *www.optimumonline.ca*, 35(4) : 68-74.

Partitioning anew the federal public service

R. Hubbard and G. Paquet. 2007. "The myth of public service as a lump of 'guardians'," *www.optimumonline.ca*, 36(1): 9-26.

| Cat's eyes: the capacity to engage intelligently

"Cat's eyes are particularly valuable in fog."
Wikipedia

C at's eye connotes raised lane markers on paved roads – two pairs of reflective glass spheres set into a rubber dome and mounted in a cast iron housing used for marking lanes, with one pair of cat's eyes showing in each direction. Patented in 1934 by Percy Shaw, this invention has done more to save lives on the road than anything since.

For this second series of our discussions with senior federal public servants, we focused our attention on one family of topics. We dealt with four challenges facing public servants in meeting the legitimate expectations of the citizenry – how to succeed in ensuring intelligent accountability, intelligent regulation, intelligent organizational design, and intelligent public service.

This chapter is about the capacity to engage fully in the fulfillment of one's burden of office both reactively and proactively, to meet obligations and to sustain commitments, when things are going well and when things are going wrong. It is no longer a matter of coping, but a matter of accepting and honouring one's burden of office.

What is called 'intelligent work' in this chapter is not easy to define. Each of the four labels (accountability, regulation, organizational design and public service) connotes both a familiar terrain and a nexus of somewhat poorly-understood and contested issues. It is not always clear what is meant by 'intelligent' when such issues are raised because the complex mechanisms behind the labels are varied and often defined in significantly different ways by the key players involved.

At the same time, whatever arrangements that have been put in place to deal with the original concern have often been used in ways that can only be called 'unintelligent' (frequently with disastrous results). Yet, most of the time, the frustrated observers have been unable to determine what would be necessary to make these arrangements more 'intelligent'. Discussions with senior executives were meant to elicit what sort of intelligent engagement would be likely to generate 'intelligent work' on all these fronts as a minimum condition if one is to meet the basic requirements of the burden of office.

A syncretic view of each theme discussed

This section provides a brief summary of the introductory statement on each topic, and a very sketchy summary view of the general substance of the conversations that followed.

Intelligent accountability

Accountability is the new mantra. It has emerged from the autopsy of recent mishaps as a panacea supposedly capable of resolving all conundrums by connecting each action and/or inaction to a source or cause to which it can be attributed, and therefore to a person or group that could be asked to render an account. Unfortunately, the world is much more complex than this simple mechanical depiction might suggest. There is not always a simple and direct connection between an outcome and a person who can be held responsible for it. As a result, accountability has become a weasel word: it has come to mean a variety of things ranging from true responsibility to the simple obligation of formally offering an official account of what has happened.

A key foundational concept at the core of the notion of accountability is the notion of the 'burden of office' on which accountability rests: what can be legitimately expected from an official. While the burden of office is relatively simple to define in a strictly hierarchical organization (to do with what the superior may legitimately expect from his subordinate), it becomes much more complex in organizations where officials have to deal with a variety of stakeholders (bosses, partners, citizens, etc.) who all have legitimate expectations that may or may not be compatible. This complex context underpins the need for 360° accountability, makes the burden of office immensely more complicated, and the notion of accountability much fuzzier – less narrowly defined and focused, less hard, less strictly financial and less manageable. This challenge has not always been acknowledged. Indeed, many officials have been in denial *vis-à-vis* this new reality, and have continued to pretend that all issues can be defined as capable of being deconstructed into cause-effect relations where officials have a unique and narrowly defined burden of office for which they have to render an account to a unique overseer.

This is the dreamland in which too many adjudicators in all sectors have chosen to live. Unintelligent accountability obviously ensues, and unfortunately, as a result, too many auditors, evaluators and adjudicators have felt empowered to declare or imply guilt and innocence willy-nilly, and to impose praise or blame somewhat speciously.

Intelligent accountability entails a more realistic appreciation of the complexity of the context, and of the complexity of the notion of burden of office that ensues. This, in turn, calls for a more diffuse and a softer notion of accountability, and one that is truly dynamic in the sense that it evolves through time. Moreover, it is not (as it has come to be in the language of auditors) the lynchpin of an *ex post* process of allocation of blame, but the basis of an *ex ante* process of social learning, capable of guiding better future action. Intelligent accountability is therefore learning accountability, soft accountability and experimentalist accountability: it is the process through which an organization in the short run must deal with deception and disinformation, and in the longer run must organize social learning in a forward-looking perspective (Paquet 2008; Patton 2011).

In the discussions, there was general agreement that accountability is too narrowly defined, and that one lives in a world of excessive rules and omnipresent watchdogs. It was also felt that common sense and trust might be brought back but that it would require action on many fronts: small steps in one's own shop, better use of training to instill the new culture of responsibility, some initiatives by communities of practices (e.g., HR, regulators, procurement) that could be instrumental in promoting a broader perspective and in finding ways to operationalize such a renewed perspective with the development and use of instruments likely to keep the watchdogs at bay. Small steps and caution were seen as mandatory in this minefield.

Intelligent regulation

Regulation is a central feature of our lives. It affects all of us daily. Yet it is poorly understood, and often has unintended consequences that make it ineffective and sometimes even toxic. These unintended consequences and other costs of regulation have led most governments to launch processes of 'regulatory reform': trying to get most of the benefits of intelligent regulation while avoiding the costs of dysfunctional regulation. These efforts have gone by many names: deregulation, smart regulation, responsive regulation, etc. Progress on these fronts has been slow.

The basic aim of all those reform movements has been a broadening and smoothening of the regulatory process: (a) an attempt to take into account the broader megacommunity in order to help it avoid ensnarement in the regulator's web; (b) a shift from hard to soft regulation, from enforcement to assistance, from reactive to preventive, and from adversarial to collaborative action, from incident-driven to problem-solving approaches; (c) a new focus on risk management that entails a new attention to impact (and not only to outcome measures), and on materiality of risk in defining priorities; (d) a recognition that this different approach is more demanding intellectually, analytically and organizationally and, therefore, much more difficult to design and to operate as a result of the effort it unrelentingly demands.

The slow evolution from traditional to smart and responsive regulation has meant a shift from a focus on more flexibility, more efficiency, more timeliness, more transparency and the use of a broader range of instruments, toward a sort of significant climbing-down of the enforcement pyramid toward less policing and more self-regulation and a focus on preventing bad things through behavioural change.

In this transformation of the regulatory process to make it more intelligent, what is involved is nothing less than a change in the nature of the task and a redefinition of the categories of harm. Such a transformation entails a much greater role for the megacommunity and for the community of practice of the regulators. But it is even more importantly a redefinition of the very nature of the regulation work: away from policing to harm reduction.

The climbing-down of the regulatory enforcement pyramid is running afoul of the trend toward more regulatory intervention in our age of distrust. Yet, the propensity to over-regulate has generally failed. The first reaction to such failures then has been to deregulate. This has not proved necessarily very satisfactory either. A second wave of reaction has been a mix of smart regulation and responsive regulation, with an emphasis on the latter.

The discussion led to the realization that the risk tolerance of Canadians may be lower than that observed in other countries. So experimenting with radical elimination of regulation (like eliminating all traffic lights as has been done elsewhere) is unthinkable. There was also much concern expressed about the focus on the 'how' of regulation instead of the 'why', and about the fixation on metrics (quantophrenia). Much hope was put in the development of communities of practice: cultivating the community of regulators would enable public servants to share best practices.

Several actions could enable regulators to do a better job: (1) allowing them to engage in discussions with their political leaders about the 'what' and the 'how' as well as about the true nature of the challenges they face; (2) increasing the scope and discretion the regulators have (pushing them to understand and accept trade-offs); (3) finding ways to provide more time and resources to engage the relevant megacommunity; and perhaps most importantly, (4) eliminating the trust-destroying philosophy of 'trust but verify' that is in good currency.

Intelligent organizational design

Organization design is to governance what engineering is to science: the essential process of operationalization without which much of the good reflective work on governance is bound to remain fruitless. Yet this design work is quite difficult, is not well done, and is likely to be a cause of governance failure and poor performance.

An organization may be x-rayed as a mix of *People* (stakeholders of all sorts with their skills, talents and responsibilities), *Architecture* (relationships of all sorts defined by the organization charts and the like), *Routines* (process, policies and procedures), and *Culture* (shared values, beliefs, language, norms and mindsets) (Roberts 2004). At any time, these components (**PARC**) are assembled within organizations in various ways – bound together by ligatures making them into a more or less coherent whole. Any shock disturbing any of these components (whether they originate within or without the organization, whether they modify a physical or a symbolic dimension) obviously triggers some realignment in all the other dimensions. So the organization continually evolves.

The main reason for effective organization design failing to materialize is probably because it is wrongly assumed that organizational design amounts to little more than tinkering with organization charts. In fact, the sort of architectural work required is immensely more demanding and commands a whole different way of thinking. It is not (and cannot be) guided by the sole sort of logic that dominates science (the search for general knowledge and the subsequent test of its validity), but by an inquiry into systems that do not yet exist:

the logic is that of disclosing and crafting a new 'world' with the sole purpose of ascertaining if it works and ensuring that it does (Romme 2003: 558).

The organization is a living entity. Buildings evolve despite their constraining structure as their occupants take hold of them, and transform their functions and missions in ways that were never planned. The same evolution occurs in organizations, but much faster and more dramatically, as a result of unintended consequences of unplanned interactions.

The role of the organization designer is to intervene, in real time in an existing assemblage, to improve the four-dimensional PARC configuration of the organization in a manner that generates better dynamic performance and resilience, given the nature of the environment in which the organization operates, but also taking into account its turbulence and its evolution, and fully recognizing the limits of such exercises.

These four dimensions may be tweaked in a creative way to provide effective dynamic coordination, but unintended consequences may thwart the whole experience. This sort of work requires: (1) a new vocabulary because critical description is crucial at the diagnostic phase; (2) a new form of knowledge, a new type of exploratory activity and a new process of experiment-based creative thinking; and (3) a new type of competencies. However, this process will lead to nothing substantial unless one has been able to develop (4) a mental tool box of levers useable in such design work and capable of guiding the tentative work of crafting new organizations. Because organization design is akin to creating a new world, none of the above will suffice unless the design process (5) truly discloses a coherent world (a body) and contributes to impart it with a style (a soul) that provides it with a sextant, focal points that underpin its being able to sustain effective coordination and change (Simons 2005; Paquet 2007).

This topic proved difficult to discuss. In large part, this likely stemmed from participants' lack of direct involvement with the process of deliberately attempting to change organizations, along with the false impression that 'organizational design' refers simply to the definitions of roles and reporting relationships. Moreover, the very notion of reorganization came with some baggage: it is often perceived as a decoy for scaling down the operations. Consequently, it often generates a culture of 'resistance to change' that tends to discourage prototyping or redesign initiatives.

Demographics were referred to as a determining factor as young people are often more willing than their older colleagues to experiment. However it was also felt that oblique strategies may be more effective as existing structures may correspond to important vested interests. The human resources function was the common ground that proved most congenial for the discussion both as a result of familiarity with the field, and as there was some agreement that this might be the locus where redesign might be regarded as a top priority.

Intelligent organizational design is not a matter of recipes but a 'way of thinking' that is non-linear, uses a holistic approach and entails the practical use of prototyping. In the case of human resources, for instance, it was felt that without (1) better information about people, (2) a more accommodating classification system, (3) a reduction in institutional rigidities and (4) the avoidance of the current mixed messages seeking both permanence and fluidity – significant improvement is going to be hard to achieve.

Intelligent public service

In a Westminster model, the public service serves elected officials by ensuring that the programs of action and inaction that the government has put in place are carried out as effectively, efficiently, economically and creatively as possible within the constraints imposed by the rule of law.

In Canada, at the federal level, the governing of the public service is carried out by a multiplicity of intermediary institutional players: Treasury Board Secretariat, Privy Council Office, Canada Public Service Agency, Public Service Commission and the Canada School of Public Service – above and beyond a myriad of actors at the departmental and agency level. It has been estimated that, at the central agency level, no less than 2,000 full-time equivalent employees are involved, and close to another 1,000 at the department and agency levels. This entails expenditures of between $300 and $400 million per year.

It has been argued that the present arrangements are far from satisfactory. The public service is often regarded as not serving elected officials well, as doing so in a rigid and not very innovative way and, therefore, as performing at a level that is below expectations. This should not be interpreted as denying in any way the general quality of the Canadian public service by comparison to the public service apparatus in other industrialized countries. It is simply that much room for improvement has been perceived by observers in a number of recent reports.

Two of those reports have been receiving much attention in recent years: the work of the Prime Minister's Advisory Committee on the Public Service (the Mazankowski-Tellier Committee) and the report of the Public Policy Forum – *Canada's Public Service in the 21st Century – Destination: Excellence* (the Ian Greene Task Force).

While these reports made a number of helpful suggestions, it is fair to say that they were both very cautious and circumspect about the way to deal with the tensions between the elected officials and the bureaucrats. They narrowly focused on human resources management issues (including performance management) that, if dealt with satisfactorily, might help the Canadian public service to perform better. Issues like the burden of office of the public service, the moral contracts binding them to the different stakeholders they serve, and the professionalism that is fundamental to their activities in our Westminster system of an independent and non-partisan public service were largely ignored. Yet those latter issues were clearly on the mind of many observers who have been wondering whether the public service in its present form can survive, and have pondered the question of what intelligent public service really means.

The discussion on this topic was painful as it is quite difficult to assume (even temporarily and for the sole purpose of discussion) that the public service (to which one belongs) might be 'unintelligent'. However it became clear as the discussion proceeded that the cumulative impact of poor accountability, regulation and organizational design could only add up to a less than perfectly intelligent public service. Again, the human resources dimension dominated the discussion because it provided more palpable evidence of the sort of dysfunction referred to in the general discussion. It provided much evidence of the difficulty of striking the 'right' balance between reliability and innovation. It also led to the recognition that there is much more need for innovation, measurement of the right things the right way, and sensible reporting.

The need for being given an 'objective not a template' and 'a goal without being told how to achieve it' were regarded as necessary prerequisites to producing good results. Mentoring and coaching were noted as quite important for improving capability. The participants deplored meaningless reporting, observing that the centre did not have the capacity to analyze all the information being sought.

In a general way, intelligent public service was seen as building on three conceptual pillars: the 'burden of office' of public servants, the many 'moral contracts' with different stakeholders, and the 'professionalism' that public servants bring to their work. Nevertheless, without a real capacity (1) for pushing back when rigid and ineffective action is ordained, (2) for cultivating communities of practice, (3) for empowering managers and (4) for measuring the right things the right way – moving toward an intelligent public service will be hard.

A personal distillation of what we learned

A cautionary statement

No conversation can make any sense without some contextual information being supplied. The conversations referred to above were held in difficult times for the Canadian public service both as a result of a troubled conjuncture (minority Conservative government after more than a dozen years of Liberal rule, decline in the trust in government and bureaucrats in general, etc.) and of a period of fundamental questioning about Canadian political institutions (*remise en question* of the role of an independent public service in dealing with elected officials in a world drifting from Big G government to small g governance and new complexity of issues as one enters an era of distrust where collaboration among a much larger number of partners is necessary but rather difficult as it remains uncharted territory, etc.).

This context could not but influence the nature of the conversations. And this turbulent environment has of necessity made it difficult to disentangle the roles of external (i.e., contextual) and internal (i.e., emerging from the fabric of the public service) factors in making sense of what was said and in explaining why such reactions were elicited by the conversations.

The temptation to ascribe much of the pathologies we observed to external factors had to be contained. Such an approach would appear to characterize senior executives of the Canadian public service as passively suffering these pressures, and without a capacity to act as *définisseurs de situation* in a learning organization. A more reasonable perspective would be to ascribe a portion of the difficulties to the complexity of the context, and a very significant portion to failures of the executives in fully mastering the technologies of survival, adaptive and generative learning.

The purpose of our conversations is obviously to foster a better understanding of the complexity of the environment and of the wickedness of the problems faced by public sector executives as well to help develop what Peter Senge calls "personal mastery" – the capacity and discipline of continually clarifying and deepening their learning process and of becoming "acutely aware of their ignorance, their incompetence, their growth areas" (Senge 1990: 142). This cannot be done without sharply identifying what one can detect as internal (behavioural and organizational) features that need to be transformed by the executives themselves.

So our clinical and provocative diagnoses have to be interpreted not as putting the onus of adjustment entirely on the executives (for there are things that will require nothing less than a modification of Canadian institutions and of the Canadian mindset), but as putting much responsibility on the senior executives' shoulders to deal with those portions of the undeniable pathologies that are under their control.

Two major contextual factors should, however, be kept in mind in interpreting what might be regarded as a stark diagnosis.

First, debates are going on about the unresolved questions about the legitimate role of the senior public servants. As Paul Thomas put it "we want an independent public service. Is this independence mainly important for the implementation of public policy to ensure fairness and impartiality in the delivery of programs and services? Is the same amount of independence required with respect to the provision of policy advice? Does independence for the public service guarantee objective advice to government? Are objectivity and independence the same quality in an institution? [...] Acceptance of the notion of a separate place in the constitutional order for an independent public service (i.e., the presumption behind Gomery and the Public Accounts Committee of the accounting officer concept) has far reaching implications. It implies, for example, that the public service has a legitimate role in helping to define the public interest." (Thomas 2008: 22-23).

In the face of such indeterminacy, it is difficult for senior executives not to be confused, and there is little anyone can do about it until some clarification materializes.

Second, the nature of the problems faced by elected officials and senior executives is immensely more complex in the world of small g governance than it used to be in the old Big G government institutional order. Yet there is a great reluctance in accepting the fact that these more wicked problems may not be capable of being handled adequately by the old artillery.

This entails a transition in the nature of the burden of office of senior executives and the development of a full acceptance that the old ways must change accordingly.

Again, the fact that this transition is far from over, and that many senior executives in the public service at all levels and many crucial partners still are in denial about the need to change significantly, cannot but paralyze action by senior executives and generate much frustration that cannot be overcome by wishful thinking.

This being said, we could not fail to observe the following perplexing phenomena as a result of our discussions.

Somebody is in charge and it is not me

A rather perplexing set of assumptions about the 'real' place of the executives in the overall governance apparatus and in the public sector cast a shadow on our conversations. One could feel a tension between the willingness by executives to take charge and to accept responsibilities for success or failures, and some sense that they are not in charge. Yet, when faced with the hypothesis that they have to take charge, because nobody is truly and completely in charge, there was a forceful reaction of disbelief.

So, the executives seemed paralyzed by the triple presumptions: (1) that it cannot be that truly nobody is in charge; (2) that since they (the executives) are not in charge themselves, (3) these 'somebodies' in charge should provide guidance.

Faced with the hypothesis that we are drifting from the world of Big G government to small g governance, the senior executives seemed unready to accept (at least initially and easily) that they are key producers of governance, that they are the ones holding the key to many of the challenges discussed. They are torn between two uncomfortable positions: the old Westminster model that tells them that they are the 'servants' of Parliament, and the new credo that claims that the super-bureaucrats and senior executives are as legitimate (in other ways) as the elected officials, and therefore should be regarded as having governing duties too.

Neither positions would seem to fit their circumstances: they simply perceive themselves as 'subordinates', and therefore as not really being in charge of anything.

This (added to the great confusion in the context) seems to have created a climate of learned helplessness that constrained even the ambit of permissible discussion to a considerable degree. Much of the casuistry displayed during the discussions (about what is success, failure, etc.) is ascribable to the fact the executives cannot bring themselves to believe that we can live in a world where nobody is in charge: they cannot, and search for some 'person in charge' either in the political sphere or in the upper sphere of the bureaucracy. This acts as a self-restraining mental prison that prevents them from claiming their rightful place in the governance structure – however constrained that place might be. How much is ascribable to the complexity of the context and how much to this mental prison is a moot point: both factors would appear to prevent the senior executives from exercising their full role of 'governors'.

One must add that this *malaise* was somewhat shaken off along the way as the different conversations proceeded. Indeed, the slow disappearance of the 'us-them' cleavage is probably one of the most positive results of the conversations conducted over the last year, especially for the younger participants: the slow evolution of a perception where the problems were being ascribed to 'them' (whomever they are), and the responses expected from 'them', toward a position reached later in the 2007-08 season, where the participants (1) came to reject that *servitude volontaire*, (2) began to recognize their share of the causal factors for the pathologies, and their responsibility in generating meaningful and effective responses, and did it in a more and more forceful way. There was no mind quake, but a significant change in mindset.

Déformation professionnelle

H.L. Mencken wrote somewhere that for every complex problem, there is a solution that is simple, clear and wrong. This is an aphorism that echoes both (1) the imperative that the degree of complexity of the discussion of or the response to an issue has to be as great as that of the issue being debated; and (2) the dangers of particularly reductive *manières de voir* that often lead specialists to be no better than any one of the blind men, in the Indian tale, trying to describe an elephant.

The prevalent mindset of executives (ascribing so much authority to external powers at least at first, and claiming so little real governance as being in their hands) explains why the executives were so reluctant to be dragged out of the concerns about the 'how' toward a better appreciation of the context, of the need to understand the 'why', and of the obligation to engage in critical and reflective thinking on these broad issues. Such a grand way of dealing with issues was simply seen as out-of-bounds.

This *déformation professionnelle* explains the impatience with contextual issues and the pleasurable satisfaction with dealing in operational details. While such a bias was not universal, it was omnipresent: enough in any case to drown efforts by many others to cast a wider net, to frame issues in a broader way and to deal with non-operational issues. This led the discussion to founder on the search for recipes and ways out, or to focus on what sounded more familiar, and more tractable aspects of the question (like human resources), instead of spawning reflections on the broader sources and causes of the problems raised. If you think that you only have a hammer, everything starts looking like a nail.

This was in no way the result of a lack of intellectual capability for the appreciation of such complexities, but rather the result of a sort of professional bias that would appear to have struck the federal executive class and drawn it away from the shoals of critical thinking into the quiet waters of operations. In a world where critical thinking is not valued as much as it used to be, and is even seen unfavourably, it is hardly surprising that in dealing with taboo topics one would be naturally led to search for a technical fix rather than for an appreciative system.

This professional bias may be ascribable to the decline in the valuation of critical thinking since the 1990s, when, in certain federal quarters of the public service, criticism became a synonym for treason. This was the time when the programs of the Canada School of Public Service were stripped of their critical edge, and when training became clearly much more focused on logistics rather than on appreciation. This bias has come to define the norms in good currency, so much so, that even groups as venturesome as the ones we met in these series of discussions tended often to shy away from tackling problems in a reflective manner to focus on instrumental and highly focalized avenues.

Cognitive dissonance

The two mental prisons mentioned above (*servitude volontaire* and *déformation professionnelle*) seem to go a fair distance in explaining the mix of cognitive dissonance, political correctness and willful blindness that marred our conversations about how to make work more intelligent. The great amount of tiptoeing around the difficult topics would appear to flow from two imperatives: avoiding any self-indictment of the public service *per se* as much as possible, and any statement that might sound politically incorrect. On the first front, this entailed much cognitive dissonance: the denial of unintelligence and of any misbehaviour by a person in bureaucratic authority was in most cases the *position de départ*, and there was much defensiveness whenever it was suggested that some particular event or some particular action might prove the point that something untoward was averred.

When the 2006 Key Leadership Competencies document was tabled showing that it was presumed that nothing untoward could be expected from the very upper ranks of the public service, the reaction was straight-faced denial that this was so until the particular pages could be shown. The examples of misbehaviour tolerated by deputy ministers and then rewarded were greeted with much *malaise* but readily dismissed as exceptions to a general diagnosis that 'things were not that bad' and that it was unreasonable to generalize on the basis of a few examples.

One could notice, even in a group that can only be characterized by all accounts as enormously more open-minded and critical than the average public sector executive, a disposition and even a propensity to defend the system by blanking out not only the implications one might reasonably derive from the observed phenomena, and also by systematically downplaying the weight of the evidence brought forth. Not only was there denial that there has been much misbehaving, but there was even some disingenuity at times in the rationalizations proposed to make sense of them.

On the political correctness front, the lines were less sharply drawn. Decades of guarded language and human rights commissions' denunciations have taken their toll. Robust language was never well received. Indeed, there was an insistence on softer language as a strategy to ensure that the issue would be dealt with. Avoiding provocative formulations was a tactic used by some not to frighten others, and for others it was tactical to de-dramatize anything untoward.

Taboo topics were defanged and the issues were degeneralized in a manner that helped to exorcise their damnable aspects. This approach allowed the group to be much bolder on the external front (then dealing with forces external to the public service) than it allowed itself to be on the internal front (i.e., when dealing with the public service proper). Still, one should note that there was a sharp contrast between the evenly balanced sub-groups – those yearning for sharp and forceful exchanges, and those hesitant about allowing it to proceed too far.

The presence of latent fear

The most elusive sense that permeated the discussions was one of latent fear.

This had nothing to do with any sort of edict but rather some form of self-censorship that has become habitual, it would seem, as a survival instinct in a world where critical thinking and sharp exchanges are no longer valued as they used to be. This is where the rampant sense of organizational violence would appear to take its toll. To a person, participants testified that *prudentia* was *de rigueur,* that it was by far the most important of the cardinal virtues in the public service these days: much more so than the other cardinal virtues – *temperentia* (the sense of limits) *fortitudo* or courage and justice. This would appear to flow from a profound culture of distrust that has come to rest within the Canadian federal public service.

This culture of distrust has much to do with the evolution of the nexus of moral contracts among the politicians, the bureaucrats, the diverse interest groups, and the citizenry as the regime drifted from Big G government to small g governance (Paquet and Pigeon 2000). In the stylized world described by people like Donald Savoie, there used to be a simple loop – linking voters to their MPs and through them to the PM and Cabinet, and then from Cabinet to ministers, departments, and the cascades of public servants back to the citizen – that has now (as he would have it) been broken (Savoie 2008). If such a loop of accountability ever existed, it is a moot point; it is clear that it has not existed for a long time, and that we have lived much more in a power matrix whose organizational chart would rather look instead like a knotted fishnet.

What has changed is the structure of moral contracts binding this set of public actors: from contracts based on trust to contracts based on distrust. Disloyalty need not be generalized for distrust to prevail: if only a small fraction of a group is disloyal but there is no way to know who they are, distrust will become endemic. Indeed, this has been the sort of drift one has observed, not only in Canada but in many advanced democracies, with the result that executives are now living in an age of distrust (Hardin 2004; Rosanvallon 2006).

This sort of distrust, together with the growth of organizational violence, is at the source of this latent fear that permeated our conversations. It is ascribable to a much greater extent than is usually blamed on poor organization design, leading to a growing gap between what is expected and what can be delivered, and consequently a source of both stress and harassment. Again, how much of it is ascribable to context (and, therefore, beyond reach for the executives interested in engineering needed repair) and how much to cultural factors within their reach (even though it might be a daunting task to deal with them) is quite difficult to ascertain.

In this context, it is therefore hardly sufficient to suggest that order can be restored only by super-bureaucrats and senior executives being given more power (as Savoie suggests). Rather, what is required, if fear is to be attenuated, is recognition that in a world of governance, new structures have to be designed and new rules of the game have to be put in place that build much more on trust than distrust.

What this refurbished system might look like has not crystallized yet but some of its contours have been sketched out by Sunstein and Thaler under the generic name of "libertarian paternalism" (Sunstein 2005: chapter 8; Thaler and Sunstein 2008). It argues for a soft, non-intrusive type of public sector intervention to nudge citizens in certain directions without forbidding, very much along the lines suggested in the governance literature.

Clearly, until such time as the very notion that 'nobody is in charge' takes hold of the mindset of public sector executives at all levels (including DMs), there is little hope that the necessary redesign will be put in place, that intelligent work will unfold, that perverse incentives, organizational violence and fear will be subdued, and that moral contracts among the different actors can be renegotiated. And, unless this can be done, there is little sense in hoping for the complete dominance of prudentia over fortitude; courage and justice will be shaken off by executives in the public service.

Conclusion

These topics deserve the attention of those who have chosen a career in the public service and find themselves less able to serve as well – to do intelligent work or to fend off perverse incentives – as they would like. Without such conversations, there may be a danger that unwittingly some of the foundational institutions that Canadians have invented to govern ourselves will be eroded. Moral contracts need to evolve constantly with circumstances, and they need to be kept in the forefront of our consciousness, if they are to be so renegotiated.

Otherwise, one may fall prey to simplistic fixes like the argument in good currency among columnists these days – *ces magistrats de l'immédiat* – that elected officials have lost legitimacy and that the 'solution' is that super-bureaucrats and senior executives need to be given more power. This sort of pretension by the managerial class is in the air in Canada and elsewhere, and it has not been critically chastised in Canada as it should be in the manner it has been in Australia (Rhodes and Wanna 2007).

References

Hardin, Russell (ed.). 2004. *Distrust*. New York, NY: Russel Sage Foundation.

Paquet, Gilles. 2007. "Organization Design as Governance's Achilles' Heel," *www.governancia.com*, 1(3): 1-11.

Paquet, Gilles. 2008. "A Plea for Intelligent Accountability," *Financial Management Institute Journal*, 19(2): 9-14.

Paquet, Gilles and Lise Pigeon. 2000. "In Search of a New Covenant" in E. Lindquist (ed.). *Government Restructuring and the Future of Career Public Service in Canada*. Toronto, ON: Institute of Public Administration of Canada, p. 475-498.

Patton, Michael Quinn. 2011. *Developmental Evaluation – Applying Complexity Concepts to Enhance Innovation and Use*. New York, NY: The Guilford Press.

Rhodes, R.A.W. and John Wanna. 2007. "The Limits to Public Value, or Rescuing Responsible Government from the Platonic Guardians," *The Australian Journal of Public Administration*, 66(4): 406-421.

Roberts, John. 2004. *The Modern Firm*. Oxford, UK: Oxford University Press.

Romme, A. Georges L. 2003. "Making a Difference: Organization as Design," *Organization Science*, 14(5): 558-573.

Rosanvallon, Pierre. 2006. *La contre-démocratie – La politique à l'âge de la défiance*. Paris, FR: Seuil.

Savoie, Donald J. 2008. *Court Government and the Collapse of Accountability in Canada and the United Kingdom*. Toronto, ON: University of Toronto Press.

Senge, Peter M. 1990. *The Fifth Discipline*. New York, NY: Doubleday.

Simons, Robert. 2005. *Levers of Organization Design*. Boston, MA: Harvard Business School Press.

Sunstein, Cass R. 2005. *Laws of Fear*. Cambridge, UK: Cambridge University Press.

Thaler, Richard H. and Cass R. Sunstein. 2008. *Nudge*. New Haven, CN: Yale University Press.

Thomas, Paul G. 2008. "Political-Administrative Interface in Canada's Public Sector," *www.optimumonline.ca*, 38(2): 21-29.

Annex: Basic documentation for each session

Intelligent accountability

J. Tussman. 1989. *The Burden of Office*. Vancouver, BC: Talonbooks.

G. Paquet. 2008. "A Plea for Intelligent Accountability," *Financial Management Institute Journal*, 19(2): 9-14.

Intelligent regulation

M.K. Sparrow. 2000. *The Regulatory Craft*. Washington, DC: The Brookings Institution Press.

W. Leiss. 2003. "Smart Regulation and Risk Management," paper prepared for the External Advisory Committee on Smart Regulation, November.

J. Graham. 2005. "Smart Regulation: Will the Government's Strategy Work?" *Canadian Medical Association Journal*, 173(12): 1469-1470.

I. Ayres and J. Braithwaite. 1995. *Responsive Regulation: Transcending the Deregulation Debate*. Oxford, UK: Oxford University Press.

Intelligent organizational design

G. Paquet. 2007. "Organization Design as Governance's Achilles' Heel," *www.governancia.com*, 1(3): 1-11.

J. Roberts. 2004. *The Modern Firm*. Oxford, UK: Oxford University Press.

A.G.L. Romme. 2003. "Making a Difference: Organization as Design," *Organization Science*, 14(5): 558-573.

Intelligent public service

G. Paquet. 1997. "The Burden of Office, Ethics and Connoisseurship," *Canadian Public Administration*, 40(1): 55-71.

Prime Minister's Advisory Committee on the Public Service. 2008. *Pursuing a High Performance Public Service*, Second Report to the Prime Minister. Ottawa, ON, February.

Public Policy Forum. 2008. *Canada's Public Service in the 21st Century: Destination: Excellence*. Ottawa, ON: Public Policy Forum.

CHAPTER 3

| Not in the catbird seat: the capacity to collibrate

> "The catbird seat is an idiomatic phrase
> used to describe an enviable position."
> *Wikipedia*

I t is not sufficient to examine the capacity to cope with a turbulent environment and to engage intelligently in challenging governance processes. These sorts of commitments remain too vague and general. Intelligent action must be more focussed and also materialize in forms that will entail some significant intervention in complex processes that no one fully controls. As we have seen, a capacity to engage is too easily neutralized by helplessness in the face of complex systems.

Consequently, one cannot presume that a simple capacity to engage will suffice. A central feature of social life in advanced industrial societies is self-policing without the constant intervention of government, because some checks and balances ensure self-balancing most of the time. This is the case in the world of governance where power, resources and information are widely distributed among many hands and heads, and nobody is fully in charge. But there is no reason to believe that such self-balancing will succeed in always ensuring resilience, innovation and fairness. Consequently, new forms of intervention in fields of social tensions may have to take the form of 'collibration' – interventions in self-balancing processes to aid one combatant or handicap another, by putting a finger on the scale to change the outcome (Dunsire 1993).

In this chapter, we focus our attention on two families of flaws in the public governance process in Canada: first, some important sources of 'unintelligence' buried (not exclusively but most importantly) in questionable if not perverse incentive reward systems – rewarding failure and deception, punishing success, positive discrimination, and failure to confront; and second, some pathologies and challenges – the propensity to develop a cult of quantification that we have called quantophrenia, the ineffectiveness of personnel performance review as a process, the puzzling notion of speaking truth to power as an ill-understood imperative, and the occlusion of cities in the national governance process.

In all such cases, some collibration is called for. Our discussions were therefore carried out at a more down to earth level, at the level of the capacity of senior executives to intervene to compensate for some difficulties that need correction if the best wayfinding is to emerge.

A syncretic view of each theme discussed

Perverse incentives

Some of the sources of the lack of intelligence noted in the last chapter are structural, others organizational, still others behavioural. We focus on some of the behavioural dimensions and particularly on toxic and perverse incentives which may help explain some of the most destructive tendencies and proclivities that would appear to undermine the governing of our social system in the private, public and social sectors: rewarding failure and deception, punishing success, positive discrimination, and failure to confront.

The issues discussed in the last chapter were not, in general, disturbing emotionally (at the end of the day, who could be in favour of unintelligent anything) and led to engaged but relatively serene discussions in all but the last session. The issues raised in the sessions we will discuss here were emotionally-loaded. A very sensitive approach was needed to deal with each of the four issues by working carefully through four stages: Is there evidence of such behaviour? Is there evidence that it has become more important of late, and that it creates problems? Can one speculate on the root causes of such behaviour? Can one design correctives in the short and longer terms?

It is fair to say that consensus was neither sought nor reached on these difficult issues. Moreover it is also true that, in general, conversations about these issues were rather difficult. Disagreement – often sharp disagreement – was recorded on all four questions about all four issues. It ranged from vibrant denial that any of these issues were relevant or had any materiality, to the sad recognition by the other half of the groups that there were rampant viral afflictions that were slowly destroying the culture of the public service as well as our social system. Our summary of these discussions is clinically sanitized in ways that try to echo the temper of the debates as fairly as possible.

Rewarding failure and deception

Incentive reward systems are foundational in organizations. When an organization sends wrong signals (as when it rewards failure and deception), it conveys to all members of the organization that performance and dedication are not required. This can only corrupt the whole incentive reward system. While one wants to be tolerant of mistakes as an essential component of the learning process, when confirmed and systematic failure and deception are rewarded by lateral moves or promotion, this can only be destructive.

The challenge is to strike the right balance: encouraging experiments, innovations (and therefore potential failures) without being seen to be rewarding gross incompetence and deception. Punishing deception is indeed the first step in establishing intelligent accountability as was explained in the discussion of intelligent accountability.

After a moment of discussion about what could be meant by 'failure' (and the need to understand that there may be some confusion and legitimate differences of opinion depending on where one stands), it was agreed that *grosso modo* rewarding failure was 'endemic'.

Why? Much was made of the extreme difficulty in dealing with poor performers, and the consequent minimal tendency for executives to keep the public interest in mind on these matters, and to take punitive action. Too often, there is a tendency to off-load problem cases by getting non-performers shunted off or promoted elsewhere. Perversely, this is often encouraged by the 'higher ups' who want to avoid the short-term havoc of quarrelsome and disruptive dismissal procedures for 'their' organization. Fear of harassment charges or of damaging personal relations encourages this culture of 'playing nice' and hyper-tolerance of failure, and it discourages criticism. Even though one may be said to live in an age when audit and oversight have become pervasive, bad results are often camouflaged and bad performers not punished. While all agreed that the private benefits of such practices are not negligible, it was also agreed that the social costs are huge.

It was felt that it is naïve to expect that there will be any change until each executive accepts that addressing this problem should be regarded as his or her own central responsibility. This requires educating persons upward that responsible action calls for (1) refusing to indulge in camouflage or beggar-thy-neighbour practices; (2) acting responsibly as a cadre of executives to reinforce this commitment; and (3) providing unfailing support to managers trying to deal with these kinds of problems.

Mechanisms or practices that help prevent such pathology from being eradicated should be questioned explicitly and raised at executive retreats. For example, it should be common knowledge and widely publicized within the organizations that harassment allegations will not be entertained if there is a performance problem. The burden of office of an executive is not first and foremost meant to be focused on being nice, but on ensuring that important public functions are performed as effectively, efficiently and creatively as possible. Those unwilling to subscribe to these principles should be relieved of their executive functions. The public expects nothing less from professional executives.

Not surprisingly, the official public service document listing key leadership competencies (a document widely used in executive training) includes two pages of 'generic' ineffective behaviours that need to be avoided by all personnel – from supervisors through deputy ministers (Government of Canada 2006). Yet, in this official document, a list of the ways of "dealing with ineffective performers" is explicitly provided *only* up to the director level: it then vanishes, as if it could not happen or even be entertained as possible at the higher level. This is perplexing especially in view of the second Mazankowski-Tellier report in which the need to "deal with poor performers" (wherever they are in the hierarchy) is singled out as particularly in need of more attention to improve performance.

Punishing success
Punishing success is even more toxic than rewarding failure. It is a form of organizational violence that indicates that personal likes and dislikes are much more important than performance. If tolerated, not only does it destroy people, but it also weakens and brings organizations down by discouraging initiative, creativity and innovation. Allowing executives to endanger the health of their organization through the pursuit of personal vendettas or sheer spite puts into question the very notion of fairness; it is no more defendable if such action is taken in order to preserve one's empire or to prevent its erosion.

Again the discussion focussed at first on the notion of 'success'. In a world of greater complexity, faster change and much pluralism, there may be some legitimate differences of opinion about what is 'success'. The general view of half the groups was that 'punishing success' was not as endemic as 'rewarding failure and deception'. Nevertheless numerous examples were cited.

There was sharp disagreement also about whether or not organizational violence (in this form or in other forms) is or is not on the rise. Some argued forcefully that it was on the rise. On the other hand, there was much denial of the problem: its reality, its increasing importance, its toxicity. The sense of denial permeated the discussion, despite the strongly held view by a plurality of participants that such denial was unconscionable.

Despite the resistance to the idea that such psychopathic behaviour may be rampant, some support was lent to the view that some *bricolage* was in order – a number of small things to make this perverse behaviour more well-known and better exposed might make it less likely. For executives, a focus on symbolic and oblique measures (e.g., referring systematically to values and ethical code) as well as 'in-your-face' demands of account in such cases may represent avenues to explore.

Even though many examples were given of individuals (Allan Cutler) having been punished for doing their job well, in a very professional way, and of organizations (Service Canada) having been savaged for questionable reasons despite award-winning experience, there was a deep reluctance to recognize that punishing success may be a viral affliction in federal public sector organizations. The assumption that senior executive officials are knights and not knaves was put forward so strongly that the very idea of entertaining the thought that success was punished seemed to be impossible for many participants to entertain.

At no time since the discussion on disloyalty (in the first series) can one say that the denial was stronger. The vocal minority was exercised by this cognitive dissonance and expressed its views sharply, but to no avail. The discussion was derailed into a philosophical disquisition on what is 'real success', and denunciations of 'pseudo-success' reached at great human costs. It is not unfair to say that some aspects of the conversation brought to mind the famous line of Lewis Carroll's Humpty Dumpty – "when I use a word, it means just what I choose it to mean." It is therefore unlikely that this conversation will have much follow-on impact.

Positive discrimination

The topic was squarely defined as *not* dealing with persons with equal capabilities on all counts but dealing different only on the basis of markers like race, gender or colour, etc.: the issue was dealing explicitly with the choice of a lesser quality candidate when candidates of higher quality are available, by-passed only because the chosen are from the minority group being targeted for positive discrimination. There is little discussion of these issues: is it because the problem does not exist or because of political correctness?

Positive discrimination (in this very particular and narrow sense) is the deliberate setting aside of key performance objectives discussed in the last two sessions (success, failure) in the name of supposedly 'higher and nobler' goals and objectives. Wittingly or not, it amounts to rewarding lesser performance and punishing higher performance in the name of some 'greater good' like making reparation for past wrongs, improving the representativeness of the bureaucracy, and the like. Moreover, it is done openly and with a great amount of self-righteousness.

There was no denial that the problem exists and is important, but it was argued that, in the public sector, one cannot be restricted to matters of efficiency or fairness: it is also a matter of legitimacy. Therefore the 'need to have a representative public service' may be legitimately used as a basis for 'corrective measures'. In other words, there was an acknowledgement that positive discrimination may be regarded as necessary in some situations in order for some barriers to be eliminated, so that one may generate a 'representative' bureaucracy.

A contrario, there was also a substantial agreement on the part of a plurality of participants that too much is made of the problem of an un-representative public service. While the structure of the public service may not match perfectly the fabric of Canadian society as it stands today (as a result of rapid demographic transformation over the last 50 years), it is unreasonable to expect instantaneous adjustments. The expertise and experience necessary for promotion to higher levels in the federal public service take time to develop. It was pointed out that market forces, demographics and time will take care of the problem (and faster than anticipated as a result of the massive retirement cohort that is forthcoming).

This suggested that perhaps positive discrimination might be overused. Some argued that it might be needed to achieve a critical mass of targeted groups to break down a systemic barrier, but, beyond that level, what is needed is simply good management of the interface at group boundaries. Nevertheless, the culture of political correctness is very strong, so that the trade-off between representativeness and efficiency-effectiveness of the public service is unlikely to be a topic that can be easily and openly discussed.

There was broad agreement that implicit discrimination (unintentional and outside the discriminator's awareness) will also require more attention.

Failure to confront

It is always unpleasant (except for sadists) to confront a person whose performance is unsatisfactory and to demand that some corrective measures be taken. Yet, it is probably the most important weakness of stewards in all sorts of organizations: the lack of capability or willingness to look a person directly in the eye and to say that 'this will not do'. Yet this is a fundamental requirement for any steward: it is part of his/her burden of office. Failure to confront is tantamount to deception, to not telling the truth, to misinforming.

The chronic unwillingness to confront may arise for many reasons. It entails, nevertheless, some reprehensible disengagement, some unacceptable strategic silence in the face of situations calling for correctives. It may also condone and nurture some 'learned helplessness' – a reaction of passivity in the face of unpleasant, harmful or damaging situations where one senses that one has neither bargaining power nor capacity to resolve the problem.

While there was a general agreement that this was a crucial problem, and that this was on the rise, there seemed to be a strong reluctance to focus any energy on designing mechanisms aimed at resolving this difficulty. The need to find ways to foster more courage was underlined, but it went no further.

Even though it was recognized that, at this time, 'strategic silence' may have become too much of a survival strategy for executives, and that it may prove very costly for organizations, relatively little in the way of positive action was argued. Yet, it was recognized that taxpayers may soon ask why they should surrender money to a state so badly equipped to exercise due diligence and to demand that public servants perform their duties efficiently, effectively and creatively, or leave.

Participants concluded that 'failure to confront' was a problem on the rise in the public service in connection with ineffective performance, but also a cause of the weakening of the challenge function with respect to policy.

Training could play a role in increasing awareness, and in teaching techniques for handling difficult conversations. Nevertheless, participants emphasized that, in many cases, people knew how to confront but that the blockages arose elsewhere – in particular, the lack of support by superiors. It was also telling that many participants found even the use of the expression like 'failure to confront' to be offensive language in Canadian culture: promoting dialogue was seen as preferable to bemoaning 'failure to confront'!

Pathologies and challenges

While the front segment of this chapter dealt with personal faults of all sorts, the latter part deals with more systemic flaws in the form of flagrant biases in perspective, of the use of flawed instruments in the conduct of governing, or of challenges unmet or met rather cavalierly in addressing issues of appropriate reporting or assuring adequate representation.

Quantophrenia

Quantification *per se* is not reprehensible. Quantitative methods have been used from time immemorial as a powerful instrument of reasoning. The problem arises when the use of such tools becomes the basis of a 'cult' roughly captured by the motto that if it cannot be measured, it does not matter. Such a cult distorts the appreciation we have of socio-economic phenomena, and this mental prison acts as blinders that have toxic, unintended consequences for public policies when they become shaped by an apparatus thus constrained.

If this happens, an unduly sanitized view of policy ensues, generating perverse incentives and increasing disrepute for program evaluation. The idea that any socio-economic measure that becomes a target becomes a bad measure is known as Goodhart's Law. Measuring a system usually disturbs it: the more precise the measurement, and the shorter its timescale, the greater the energy of the disturbance, and the greater the unpredictability of the outcome (Hoskin 1996).

Many examples were offered of the toxicity of Goodhart's Law: fixation on quantified benchmarks that had perverse effects (e.g., steering decisions on the basis of measurements rather than whether it serves a purpose), and turning attention away from either maintaining professional quality or doing real work in order to focus on 'feeding the beast', i.e., the administrative machine demanding numbers.

Pointed pressures for ever more rigid accountability (e.g., to provide elaborate defenses of choices and effectiveness to political masters or the Office of the Auditor General) generate a futile attempt to impose a command-and-control system on an increasingly complex and unpredictable world that requires ever more flexibility and the capacity to adapt to rapidly changing circumstances if the necessary social learning is to be enabled. This had led to much energy and time being expended to 'find' particular concrete (numerical) evidence to support a choice once made, rather than on implementing the best possible response as effectively and efficiently as possible.

A good deal of quantophrenia is self-imposed by the bureaucracy: not by either politicians or the public. Why? Perhaps it is nothing more than a futile attempt to look scientistic in order to minimize the likelihood of blame. An example is the Treasury Board Secretariat's 2005 Management Accountability Framework (MAF). It originated in the development of two simple gauges for service delivery: (1) Are the service deliverers relatively happy with the service process and their part in it? and (2) Are those receiving the service relatively satisfied with it? But this innocuous pair of questions has grown into a monstrously complex exercise in quantophrenia. Even though it has been said that the MAF process has improved as a tool over the years, and that it has been found to be robust as an assessment process by an independent evaluation in 2009, there was no correlation between departmental investment in MAF and MAF performance. The real challenge is to engage in an evidence-based exploration of issues (wherever the evidence is and whatever form it takes) without relying exclusively on a numerical representation of reality, thus diverting public servants' attention towards artificial targets and away from doing their job as effectively as possible.

Opinion was divided over the likelihood of things changing relatively soon: many felt that this mania would eventually fade away as earlier experiences showed (*pace* PPBS); others felt that generation Y public servants would simply leave rather than get bogged down in such nonsense, and thus change might become inevitable relatively soon.

Notwithstanding the difficulties, the legitimate pressure from citizens wanting value for money and politicians demanding to know if the right thing is being done the right way, mean that ways need to be found to improve performance in a world in which 'no one is in charge'. This means putting in place instruments to gain a sense of the overall direction (e.g., east or west) and then allowing much more self-steering of the vehicle by partners (depending on context), but with consequences for those responsible if the vehicle gets and stays 'off the road'.

There is already some 'push back' with respect to the MAF: for example, agents of Parliament creating a 'common front' and refusing to report some things to the centre; managers who have acquired more authority under recent Human Resources Modernization arrangements presenting clear and timely explanations to defend their judgments rather than subjecting themselves to the quantophrenic exercises that some try to inflict on them.

An alternative to quantophrenia (for an alternative is necessary) might be an 'ergonomic' approach – focus on continuous improvement by providing easily learned and implemented tools that focus attention on possibilities for action aimed at the real problem to be solved (like checklists in operating rooms that have been shown to reduce both avoidable deaths and follow-on complications by 35-40 percent) (Gawande 2009).

Performance review

A critical review of the Performance Measurement Agreement (PMA) in use has shown that its effectiveness depends on how it is used. A knowledgeable expert in good human resources management could increase the likelihood that on-going key commitments are realistic and well spelled out, and that bosses and subordinate executives are enabled to have constructive discussions about achievements as well as about 'goodness of fit' between person and context (not simply concluding that someone was a 'poor performer' in general). But this is in no way the general experience with the personnel performance review.

Participants pointed both to the futility of trying to stimulate regular boss-subordinate discussions using the PMA, and to the distortion effects flowing from the way it was used for determining performance pay. Mostly the instrument in use tends to focus on ensuring boxes are checked mentioning that the discussion has occurred and the required discussions were held before a specified date – rather than focusing on the substance of the communication to ensure that good results were achieved. The efforts to justify a boss's decision (to peers, higher ups etc.) are often more important than the PMA scores. The PMA becomes a lengthy distraction from both the organization's real results and the necessary boss-subordinate discussions. Moreover, insistence on hard percentages of over and under performers at the top and bottom of the scale, and consequential pay at risk, regardless of the size of the organization or the nature of demands put upon it, can (and do) lead to 'game playing' and perverse incentives.

Culbert (2008) has proposed a two-sided, reciprocally accountable, negotiated performance preview as an alternative to the traditional performance review – that he scathingly calls a "mainstream practice that ... is negative to corporate performance, an obstacle to straight-talk relationships, and a prime cause of low morale at work."

Generally participants felt that Culbert's assessment of the downsides of performance review echoed (albeit in radical language) some of their concerns, and that the idea of a performance preview with its two-way accountability had some merit. In fact, some but not enough good and regular boss-subordinate conversations are taking place. What appears to be needed is a combination of hard and soft measures, of prospective and retrospective views, possibly using a rolling timeframe that extends beyond one fiscal year.

It was observed that effective performance is often ascribable to the organizational culture. The nature of the work and the organization's history are also important. An enriched, evidence-based exploration of performance issues before, during and after the fact, needs to be the focus of effective performance management if it is to enable and support necessary organizational innovativeness, nimbleness and resilience.

Speaking truth to power

'Speaking truth to power' is a sanctimonious-sounding phrase that is often used today to remind senior public servants of their burden of office – to serve the government of the day (subject to the laws of the land) first and foremost by speaking truth to elected officials. Some see it as an arrogant, value-laden and self-serving stance: public servants requiring all to assume that they are in possession of the truth, the only truth, and as such charged with the duty of enlightening the unenlightened. Others avoid reflecting on the nature of this stance and focus only on the challenges of telling people what they may not wish to hear.

While there is no doubt that politicians and bureaucrats have possibly different legitimate views of the public interest (the former's legitimacy being based on their electoral support; the latter's based on some form of expertise) and there is a need for these different views to be merged in some way, it is pretentious to assume that the bureaucrat's views represent a superior, untainted truth, and should trump the politicians' views, which is by definition seen as tainted.[6]

Some view the duty of the bureaucrat as purely informational (making the politician aware of what the bureaucrat feels to be the public interest); others perceive this duty as a duty to influence the politician's view so as to have the bureaucrat's view prevail; still others see the challenge as a duty to ensure the best blurring and blending of these two perceptions of the public interest (when they are in conflict) through an imaginative reframing that enables the crucial aspects of both views to be preserved – in the search for superior solutions likely to serve the citizenry best. In today's world, fraught with mistrust, carrying out that burden of office in the third sense may be particularly difficult.

Trust is a central feature in this process of reconciliation of different views of the public interest. Forceful confrontation may be useful at times, but using imagination may be a much better way to deal with the search for superior solutions through alignment of interests, benevolent concern, competence and integrity. What senior bureaucrats require to fulfill their burden of office (i.e., speaking truth to power) is primarily courage (Hubbard 2009).

The bureaucrat's burden of office does not entail staring down the elected officials but rather (in virtually all cases) reframing issues so as to make the views of politicians and bureaucrats compatible. It requires a new mindset, some new principles and some new mechanisms. The political-bureaucratic relationship has been aptly compared to the relationship between a wife and her mother-in-law – both loving the husband/son but each defining 'love' in a different way, and having to find some way to rub along together as a result. For the political-bureaucratic relationship, the common interest is the public interest, and constructive ways must be found to manage the natural tension between different views of the public interest for the sake of the citizen.

[6] Yet this remains a view in good currency and even an article of faith in some federal bureaucratic circles. For an exposé of its resilience in the recent past, see Gilles Paquet, 2013.

The transformation of our governance system towards one that is collaborative rather than strictly hierarchical has begun in earnest, so that dealing upwards (with political or bureaucratic bosses) has become an exercise in finding effective ways to create a new frame setting out the public interest: one that is a blending of the separate views (e.g., political and technical), into a 'super'-vision (a more comprehensive vision than the ones held by the different parties) in order to get both parties to see what they cannot see separately on their own.

What role for cities in public governance?

Canada is a nation of cities. And yet, in the Canadian governance scheme, cities are occluded. Even though most citizens live in cities (50 percent in the four largest cities in Canada; close to 75 percent in the largest 25 cities) and receive most of their daily public sector benefits at this level, this level of governance is starved for resources and prevented from playing its role by very rigid restrictions on the range of powers that it can exercise.

There are feeble signs that this is slowly changing as some Canadian cities acquire city charters. But, *de facto*, the invisibility of cities in the public governance system of the country is a measure of the system's incapacity to take into account the new realities. How much of what is done at the federal and provincial levels could be effectively delegated to cities? What would be necessary to bring it forth in key areas? Where should we start? What would it mean for federalism?

A large number of national concerns and issues are defined and lived in an urban context. Cities are not only the engines of economic prosperity, but also where Canadian society and polity thrive. Yet, a silly mental prison would appear to suggest that, because provinces utilized their powers to establish cities, this entails the servitude of cities as creatures of the provinces in perpetuity.

Reframing our notion of fiscal federalism to include and engage fully the city level is an obvious solution, and already some proposals have been put forward that would allot to cities a portion of the sales tax and of the personal and corporate income taxes (the Winnipeg proposals). But there is also a need to modernize the governance framework of cities in order to give them a broader range of powers defined not by general municipal acts but by stand-alone charters known as city charters. A new set of arrangements inspired by subsidiarity would appear to respond well to the present needs.

Provinces have resisted such moves. The federal government has of late begun to transfer more and more resources not to cities as such but to urban corporations (universities), other entities, and individuals at the local level – doing an end-run around the provinces. It is bound to increase with the series of national infrastructure programs. A sort of hourglass federalism is in the making: the federal government trying to retain as much power as possible, but also to enter into non-formalized arrangements to bolster the authority and resource base of the cities. This is generating staunch opposition from the provinces.

A personal distillation of what we learned

This set of issues pertains to various pathologies of governance for which subtle interventions of collibration would appear to be called for – interventions at the behavioural, cognitive and organizational levels. Yet, there would appear to be strong undercurrents of resistance that are likely to prevent the requisite interventions.

Moral vacancy
All the perverse incentives examined in the early sessions of this phase of our discussions referred to forms of ethical failures of one sort or another. Most of them have been the result of bad habits that are clearly forms of lies, unfairness and deceit, and have become the new norms over time in our world of moral relativism.

What was most difficult to understand was the relative insensitivity of participants to these forms of dishonesty, and the extent to which they have been reluctant to denounce starkly their having become normal practice. This was the case despite a clear understanding that these practices could only be destructive for the legitimacy of public institutions. Indeed, the intellectual acrobatics, displayed to rationalize such practices, suggest that very few participants may have come out of those discussions with a commitment to fight such perverse ways.

Some such schemes like positive discrimination may be defended in the name of some ideals, but rewarding failure, punishing success, and failure to confront have no such backstop defence. They represent dishonourable and cowardly practices that can only destroy the credibility of institutions, and the trust necessary for our organizations and institutions to perform their tasks. Yet, not only was there a denial that such practices are in good currency, and that they are becoming more important strictly for convenience sake, but one could detect no sense of outrage in the face of such abhorrent practices. Nor was there in any of the sessions any sense of a commitment to relentless persistence to eradicate such practices. Much more time was spent denying the importance of such practices and rationalizing them than one might have expected.

More than in most other sessions, one had the impression that the moral sense had been completely eroded: expediency, convenience-first, and an immense lack of courage (when there seemed to be no other reason to indulge in such practices) were at no time denounced. Learned helplessness generated not only cognitive dissonance but also moral numbness, and seemed to obliterate any sense that there was a need to interfere to stop dishonourable practices.

One may ascribe such reactions to the prevalent moral relativism, but there was also a whiff of fatalism in this attitude that tends to accept that anything goes, and that there is not much one can do about it, even though this would appear to be in such clear violation of the burden of office of senior executives in the public sector who are expected to perform at level five in Kolhberg's scale – i.e., honouring all moral contracts that call for dealing fairly and honestly with all partners. How can one expect effective collibration activity from senior executives when the very capacity to recognize dishonourable acts as punishable would appear to have evaporated?

This deliquescence of the moral sense and of the categorical imperative that one cannot be silent in the face of such immoral practices is not a phenomenon restricted to senior public sector executives. Gary Caldwell (2012) has noted that the duty to come to the rescue of fellow members of the community is disappearing in Canada.[7] It would appear that in the face of abuse and dishonourable behaviour, the response is compliance and escape. One could not fail to detect the same fatalism and learned helplessness in those sessions.

The fact that the Canadian common public culture would appear to have allowed this same sort of lack of courage to become common place cannot easily be used to defend the same sort of deliquescence in the ranks of Canadian federal senior executives of the public sector. All Canadians may breathe the same air, but the burden of office of senior executives is heavier than that of ordinary citizens because their learned helplessness triggers more toxic consequences than the inactions of ordinary blokes.

* * * *

Fortunately, the second group of topics dealt within this phase of our work did not lead to such depressing conclusions. Quantophrenia and personnel performance review pertained to 'flawed instruments' that have had a negative impact and an unfortunate steering effect on public sector governance: the propensity to quantulate generating, in both cases, a fixation on very imperfect measurements instead of promoting a better use of judgment. The final two topics (speaking truth to power and the occlusion of cities) revealed different forms of 'schizophrenia' emerging from a failure to understand systems and resulting in governance failures:

---

[7] Caldwell dedicates his book to Sarto Roy, a student at Polytechnique "who committed suicide out of remorse for having done nothing to stop the December 1999 massacre at which he was present ... May his gesture not be entirely in vain" (Caldwell 2012, dedication page). Roy's remorse would not appear to have struck many of the other men present who chose to make use of the moments when the killer (who was shooting only women) was recharging his gun not to attempt to stop him, but to escape.

(1) an inability to effectively merge the contributions of the different types of officials (elected officials, bureaucrats, but also citizens as producers of governance) and, as a result, poor collaboration and governance failures; and (2) an inability to recognize the need to give an adequate role for cities (occlusion and exclusion) in public governance as a result of a reluctance to decentralize the governance of the country. This reluctance is well documented at both the federal and provincial levels, but the denial of a larger role for cities is largely ascribable to the centralized mindset of the provinces. These two families of pathologies of governance (ascribable to flawed instruments and schizophrenia) are deeply rooted in crippling epistemologies, and in a deep risk aversion and fear of experimentation.

Crippling epistemologies

Gerd Gigerenzer has underlined the important differences between topic-oriented and discipline-oriented research (2008: v-vi). The latter sort is rooted in an angle of vision that may be quite crippling as it systematically limits what is considered as relevant knowledge, and leads to a reductive representation of reality. One would have expected practitioners of public management to have a natural tendency to work *à la* Dewey in a topic-oriented way, and to insist on the guidepost – "In the beginning is the issue". This unfortunately proved not to be the case.

Scientism (after having perverted many of the social sciences over the last decades, and having imposed a reductive framework on their activities) would appear, of late, to have succeeded in pervading the field of public administration. It has thereby imposed an artificial notion of rationality on the operations of the public household: a norm of idealized technical rationality or optimization under constraint where a notion of 'ecological rationality' (the co-evolution between heuristics and environments) has traditionally been perceived as much more adequate, and therefore warranted (Vickers 1965; Gigerenzer 2008: 8).

The seduction of quantophrenia and the ambition of constructing an idealized numerical model of the public household have been the result of the ambition to apply management science and operations research approaches (that have proved useful in handling logistics and well-structured problems of service delivery) to the ill-structured and much fuzzier edifice of public policy. Such an elaborate ethereal (idealized and sanitized) model is put forward as a substitute for the messy reality out there (McCormack 2008).

The dual process of sanitized models and of exclusive reliance on quantitative indicators has 'cartoonized' the public administration process. There is nothing inherently wrong about simplifying, in a meaningful way, a complex process for analysis, or quantifying anything that can meaningfully be quantified. The downside of the quantophrenic modelling cosmology becomes toxic when quantification becomes a camouflage or verges on being a mystification, because it is used to sweep under the carpet unpleasant intractable issues while focusing attention on a reductive vision of the policy process. This is not unlike the pretensions of those naïve psephologists claiming to give an adequate account of power politics and political behaviour through counting votes. It is not unlike pretending to build meteorology "on elaborate computations of the flutterings of flags" (Andreski 1974: 132).

It is natural for academics to fall prey to this mode of thinking – they have always been *terribles simplificateurs*! It is less obvious how hordes of practitioners have come to be mesmerized by this reductive way of thinking. While the massaging of numbers probably provides much intellectual satisfaction to massagers, and may provide a comfort zone for operatives who can use them to immunize themselves from blame, the process can easily degenerate into an exercise in the management of a fictional numerical representation of reality, rather than remaining an effort to painfully nudge reality into a preferred direction.

The discussion of quantophrenia and performance review revealed that crippling epistemologies have taken hold of a significantly important portion of the upper echelon of the Canadian public service. In the post-Gomery world, quantophrenia has become a security blanket for public servants under surveillance. Consequently, even if such exercises are regarded as mostly futile and rather costly in terms of resources required, executives simply have bowed to the edicts from above, and developed the habit of filling the required forms 'creatively' so as to keep the 'beast' satisfied. Creatively is the operative word in the last paragraph: we were informed that MAF numbers are not only massaged but manufactured and/or invented.

To the extent that it has remained possible to keep these fictions from interfering too much with the real work, it may be said to represent nothing but an additional element of waste. To the extent that this mindset triggers perverse steering effects, the costs of these crippling epistemologies in derailing policies or in generating governance failures can be enormous (Paquet 2009a, b).

Middle-ranked EXs are trying to immunize themselves against the new quantulators. This requires much *fortitudo* (a capacity to take into account context and long term) and some scheming virtuously. In particular, foot dragging is quite popular. As Georges Brassens would put it, *"mourir pour des idées bien sûr, mais de mort lente"* – for new ideas turn out not to be in good currency for long, and often the same language is used to propose and dispose of the same apparatus.[8]

Risk aversion and fear of experimentation

One of the immense costs of those fictional representations of the social system is that, for survival sake, the whole public service at the mid-ranked EX level may have been driven to a state of suspended animation. Having succeeded in keeping the quantulation machine at bay through sheer creativity, and knowing that good scores may do no more than ensure peace but that bad scores entail retribution, there is a likelihood of

---

[8] It would appear that the spirit of 'streamlining' can be used to explain both the creation and the dismantling of the Canada Public Service Agency (2003, 2009).

an increase in risk aversion and in fear of experimentation – matters that the new metrics are unlikely to pick up and most unlikely to value positively – will materialize.

Indeed, experimentation is explicitly discouraged if it is creating disturbances in any way. It is especially meaningful as a deterrent to innovation when it comes to efforts to accommodate diversity of preferences or to foster new forms of collaboration. For in such cases, the heavy costs of revamping the system (while ensuring satisfactory MAF results) may be sufficient to kill innovation altogether.

The whole importance of a redefinition of the notion of speaking truth to power as calling for more imagination than courage, and for the need to invent new ways of making the federal apparatus more inclusive and more innovative, may help to realize the full extent of the chilling effect that the quantophreniacs inflict on the system.

In neither of these last two discussions (the politicians-bureaucracy and federal-provincial-local interfaces) – despite the central importance of overcoming crippling schizophrenia – was there any appetite for executives to indulge in experimentation. Indeed, it became quite clear that EXs did not feel that these issues were in any way on their radar screen. It is as if the machinery of government was regarded as arrested in time, and their burden of office had nothing to do with the organizational redesign of arrangements that are regarded as dysfunctional.

In fact, the whole notion of collaborative governance – and its core concern about designing new technologies of cooperation (Saveri et al. 2005) – would appear to have ceased to be of concern to EXs. They would appear to take the structures as givens, and only envisage their responsibility as operating smoothly within these structures. Organizational design does not appear to fall within their jurisdiction.

In the mid-ranked federal EX cadre, it would appear that the challenges of design have come to be regarded as the sole prerogative of some higher-ups (whoever they may be) and not part of the ongoing responsibility of all EXs.

Most certainly, the post-Gomery accountability craze and the chilling effect it has generated have done much to reinforce this sort of disengagement.

Conclusion

The story of this third phase in our discussions has been on the whole rather sad.

The first segment of these discussions revealed a significant unwillingness to admit the prevalence of perverse incentives and reprehensible behaviours, and little taste to do anything substantive to eradicate or even to denounce these dishonourable and immoral practices. While it would be irresponsible to generalize in any way from our very small universe, the general impression of helplessness that transpired on these topics was in such sharp opposition to the sort of constructive discussions carried out on other topics that we were forced to concede that we had trespassed on some taboo land.

There may be issues on which senior executives can express fully their discontent; these were not in the realm of the discussable, not even when dishonest and dishonourable practices were put on the table, and evidence apposed.

The same sort of disengagement was recorded in relation to the second segment about pathologies and challenges. But the issues being more technical than moral, the diffidence appeared equally reprehensible but in some way more defendable. In both cases, however, it most certainly revealed a tamed critical sense and an unwillingness to engage in bold speculation about modifications to the social architecture of the federal arrangements.

Whether this sort of diffidence about engaging in anything but the functioning of the machinery of government reveals a long-term steady state, or whether it is the result of the closing of the public service mind by the extraordinary circumstances generated by the Gomery inquiry and the numbing impact of the financial crisis in the winter of 2009, cannot be ascertained at this time.

The degree of anomie in the federal public service system has undoubtedly grown in the last while, and it is hardly surprising that, in times of crisis, quantification as a rampart against attacks, and hyper-prudence when dealing with institutional change are easy to understand. This may be also a result of battle fatigue: the dual shocks of the recession and of the political instability of the minority government may have forced EXs to keep their noses closer to the grindstone.

The complexity of the logistical aspects may have become such that anything with a whiff of philosophical content has been deleted from the priority list. Moreover, so many EXs are going to retire in the next while that it may be that they are unwilling to question, in public, many of the assumptions and practices they might question in the privacy of their homes. If this is the case, one may regard the despondency observed as a temporary phenomenon.

Some say overoptimistically that there is some ground to believe that this represents a demographic moment. Supposedly, the spirit of the new cohort is already making itself known, and it would appear to be more subversive if one is to believe some of the mottos they brandish – like "scheming virtuously" (Charney and Mangulabnan 2008). However, occasions to meet EXs in executive development contexts over the last while have forced us to temper this sort of optimistic wishful thinking. The palpable distaste these days in such classes for any sort of difficult intellectual analysis of the changing landscape, the unquenchable taste for stories, and the sense conveyed to presenters that participants should not be forced to deal with anything difficult to understand, that executive development is largely an entertaining and interesting light presentation, show and tell, and tourism – all this has been so flagrant that we have had to stop fantasizing about a new renaissance.

References

Andreski, Stanislav. 1974. *Social Sciences as Sorcery.* Harmondsworth, UK: Penguin.

Caldwell, Gary. 2012. *Canadian Public Culture.* Ste-Edwidge-de-Clifton, QC: The Fermentation Press.

Canada Public Service Agency. 2003. "As part of the streamlining of the Treasury Board Secretariat, a new Public Service Human Resource Management Agency of Canada will be established," December 12, (http://epe.lac-bac.gc.ca/100/205/301/prime_minister-ef/paul_martin/05-10-06/www.pm.gc.ca/eng/news.asp@id=2).

Canada Public Service Agency. 2009. "Prime Minister Stephen Harper today announced changes to streamline and improve the management of human resources in the Public Service of Canada," February 6, (http://pm.gc.ca/eng/media.asp?category=1&id=2413).

Charney, Nicholas and Mike Mangulabnan. 2008. *Scheming Virtuously: A Handbook for Public Servants,* www.cpsrenewal.ca.

Culbert, S.A. 2008. "Get Rid of the Performance Review!" *The Wall Street Journal,* October 20, R4.

Dunsire, Andrew. 1993. "Manipulating Social Tensions: Collibration as an Alternative Mode of Government Intervention," Discussion Paper 93/7. Köln, DE: Max-Planck-Institut für Geselschaftsforschung.

Gawande, Atul. 2009. *The Checklist Manifesto – How to Get Things Right.* New York, NY: Metropolitan Books.

Gigerenzer, Gerd. 2008. *Rationality for Mortals.* Oxford, UK: Oxford University Press.

Government of Canada. 2006. *Key Leadership Competencies.* Ottawa, ON: The Public Service Human Resources Management Agency of Canada and the Public Service Commission.

Hoskin, Keith. 1996. "The 'awful idea of accountability': inscribing people into the measurement of objects" in R. Munro and J. Mouritsen (eds.). *Accountability: Power, Ethos and The Technologies of Managing.* London, UK: International Thomson Business Press, p. 265-282.

Hubbard, Ruth. 2009. "Speaking Truth to Power: A Matter of Imagination and Courage," *Canadian Government Executive,* January, 10-11.

McCormack, Lee. 2008. *Institutional Foundations for Performance Budgeting: The Case of the Government of Canada.* Ottawa, ON: Canadian Comprehensive Auditing Foundation.

Paquet, Gilles. 2009a. *Scheming virtuously: The road to collaborative governance.* Ottawa, ON: Invenire Books.

Paquet, Gilles. 2009b. *Crippling Epistemologies and Governance Failures.* Ottawa, ON: The University of Ottawa Press.

Paquet, Gilles. 2013. "The Political-Bureaucratic Interface: a comment on Andrew Griffith's expedition," *www.optimumonline.ca,* 43(4): 61-74.

Saveri, Andrea et al. 2005. *Technologies of Cooperation.* Palo Alto, CA: Institute for the Future.

Vickers, Geoffrey. 1965. *The Art of Judgment.* London, UK: Methuen.

Annex: Basic documentation for each session

Rewarding failure and deception

O. O'Neill. 2002. *A Question of Trust*. Cambridge, UK: Cambridge University Press.

Punishing success

G. Paquet and L. Pigeon. 2000. "In Search of a New Covenant" in E. Lindquist (ed.). *Government Restructuring and the Future of Career Public Service in Canada*. Toronto, ON: Institute of Public Administration of Canada, p. 475-498.

Positive discrimination

G. Paquet. 2006. "APEX 2006 Two-Tracked Symposium: A Curmudgeon's Commentary," *www.optimumonline.ca*, 36(2): 54-62.

M. Bertrand et al. 2005. "Implicit Discrimination," *American Economics Association Papers and Proceedings*, May, p. 94-98.

Failure to confront

C. Peterson et al. 1993. *Learned Helplessness*. New York, NY: Oxford University Press.

K.L. Stewart. 2002. "Confrontation – Some Practical Guidelines for Confronting Others Effectively," a presentation for the SOCM Physician Leaders' Forum, April 25.

T. Lenski. 2006. "7 Fears of Confronting Conflict," http://lenski. com/7-fears-of-confronting-conflict/, April 7.

Quantophrenia

G. Paquet. 2009. "Quantophrenia," *www.optimumonline*, 39(1): 14-27.

Performance review

S.A. Culbert. 2008. "Get Rid of the Performance Review!" *The Wall Street Journal*, October 20, R4.

Speaking truth to power

R. Hubbard. 2009. "Speaking Truth to Power," *Canadian Government Executive*, 15(1): 10-11.

C. Wilson. 2007. "Facilitating Contingent Collaboration," *www.optimumonline.ca*, 37(1): 1-8.

What role for cities in public governance?

M. Harcourt. 2006. *From restless communities to resilient places.* Final Report. Ottawa, ON: External Advisory Committee on Cities and Communities.

CHAPTER 4

| The unwisdom of cats: the capacity to reframe

"In a cat's eye, all belong to cats."
English proverb

One could not emerge from the depressing last series of discussions reported in chapter 3 without an urge to extract oneself from the sense of fatality and helplessness with which one was left. The topics for the final series of meetings were chosen to force the discussions onto the design stage – however uncomfortable the participants may have felt about issues of reframing and of social architecture in earlier sessions. A clear sub-objective was to test whether, in discussions about reframing, the participants would reveal the same diffidence that had emerged when our invitation to collibrate in a significant way was extended to them in the last chapter.

The capacity to reframe is at the core of the innovation process: a different *manière de voir* is at the source of new approaches and new technologies of collaborative governance (Hubbard and Paquet 2013). It requires different intellectual skills mobilizing imagination and prospecting *futuribles*. Our sense was that difficult and provocative topics like the need to redesign various key components of public administration to generate effective collaborative governance might prompt participants to deal with the longer run.

A syncretic view of each theme discussed

The political-bureaucratic interface

This theme had been dealt with ever so lightly in the early part of chapter 2, but our intent here was to set the stage for a broader debate about the way our institutions might have to be redesigned if the drift from Big G (government) to small g (governance) were to succeed in generating new and more performing sets of institutions for this new context.

Both politicians and bureaucrats are legitimate officials: the former draw their legitimacy from elections as representatives of the citizens, and the latter from competitions that have confirmed their expertise and professionalism for particular sets of responsibilities. Both groups may have views about the public good and the public interest that may be at variance. However, what is not always as clear as it should be is how a blend of both perspectives is to be arrived at.

Some brandish the Westminster philosophy to remind everyone that, in the final analysis, the politicians should have the ultimate say, and that bureaucrats should serve them loyally. Others view the public service as the "Platonic guardians of the public interest" and of the Constitution against the claims of 'responsible government', and as echoing a truer version of the public interest than what the politicians can come up with. Indeed it is said by some that the loyalty of the public servant to government and minister is secondary to the loyalty to the institution of the public service itself! A third group argues that these polar-opposite positions are too absolute, and that mechanisms have to be found to ensure that workable and effective collaboration materializes between both groups (and all sorts of third parties) through negotiated compromises.

In a world where the level of mutual understanding and trust on both sides appears to have declined significantly in the recent past (Paquet and Pigeon 2000; Paquet 2010), the 'traditional' bargain between politicians and bureaucrats (non-partisanship, loyalty, impartiality, discretion and professionalism provided by bureaucrats in exchange for anonymity and security of tenure) has been broken. As a matter of consequence, the interface must be redefined, but whether it should be as a result of revisited conventions or of rewritten legislation is not clear. What is not always clear either is how bureaucrats are to ensure a right balance between responsiveness and loyalty on the one hand, and independence and impartiality on the other.

Participants were explicitly invited to reflect on what the new design of public sector arrangements should look like to respond to the new challenges, but, despite pressure, they would not bite. Whether it was because they had nothing to say about it or whether they were not interested in such issues remains unclear, but whatever might be the reason, this can only be a cause for concern.

Participants pointed to many important factors that have contributed to the erosion of the traditional bargain. Some of these factors are 'externally' generated – such as the greater complexity of the issues and the greater possibility of honest differences of opinions arrived at on the basis of mountains of information of varying credibility, and citizens demanding more say in policy making. Others are the result of 'internally' generated factors – such as the more limited face-to-face interaction between politicians and bureaucrats as well as a decline in basic civility in their encounters, the fast-paced 'churn' in senior ranks that has reduced the reservoirs of deep technical expertise available in strategic positions in certain issue domains (making creativity more difficult), the loss of some capacity to think critically, and constrained budgets (e.g., limiting travel, consultation and resources for educating publics) that impede the enriched relational connections necessary for effective exchanges between politicians, bureaucrats and the citizenry.

These factors are over and above (a) the understandable deep mistrust of the public servants in place when a new party takes power after many years in opposition, and (b) the pressure of permanent campaigning as the new regime of elected officials that is pushing ministers to 'do something quickly', so that if the public service has nothing to offer immediately, the minister has to improvise and find advice wherever s/he can. Such tensions can only add to the difficulty of collaborating.

In the United Kingdom, two robustly enforced initiatives were announced a while back – one reminding ministers to listen carefully to the advice of their public servants, and another underscoring the importance of public servants providing complete, accurate and timely information to ministers, Parliament and the public. While such a system-wide and public restatement of fundamental principles has not happened in Canada, it was felt that there might be a need for it.

Finally, the emergence of more and more super-bureaucrats (Auditor General and other agents of Parliament) who have allowed themselves to interpret their mandate as being the guardian/conscience/keeper/challenger of the politicians and of the other bureaucrats, and have been celebrated by some academics for doing so, has muddied the water even more by inviting the ordinary bureaucrats to feel legitimate in questioning whether loyalty to their political masters was ever a virtue.

Very much as in the case of the reluctance to use their capacity to collibrate, there was a great reluctance on the part of senior executives to come forth with suggestions as to how one might reframe and redesign what was regarded by all as flawed arrangements. This quasi-systematic refusal to regard organizational redesign as part of their burden of office has led the participants to regard our invitation to reframe as an exercise entirely of fantasy. Indeed, this is the attitude that prevailed during the discussions about the four topics of this last phase of our conversations. To the extent that the participants got engaged, it was too often at a very superficial level, and their suggestions to reframe and redesign were somewhat trite and banal.

In fact, the participants responded to an invitation to reframe, to innovate and to redesign by suggestions that were more in the nature of innocuous interior redecoration: better use of 'competitive intelligence' (as the private sector organizations do), better sifting of information in terms of reliability and credibility, distilling the main points of view emerging from a confusing plethora of voices more effectively, and developing improved ways to engage groups across the country and to network with them. There was also some mention of the importance of building new loci for dialogue if the necessary trust is to be rebuilt.

The federal public service as a nexus of moral contracts

The second sessions were designed to draw attention to specific aspects of the duties of the public servants – the moral contracts defining their burden of office. The texture of the Canadian federal public service was not approached as a management challenge as was done in chapter 2, but as a nexus of a variety of moral contracts of which the political-bureaucratic bargain is only one.

The world of governance has become more complex, the environment more turbulent, and, given the wide distribution of information, power and resources among many persons and groups, no one can be said to be fully and solely 'in charge'. This means that all (including the bureaucrats) must have rapport and interaction with many parties in the process of governing. This entails the involvement of most officials in multiple moral contracts and, therefore, the need to honour multiple loyalties. The collaborative governance process that has emerged (including more actors, more consultation and negotiation, more horizontal and transversal partnerships, etc.) has transmogrified public administration.

Yet, many officials are in denial *vis-à-vis* the fact that top-down, Big G government is being displaced by small g, bottom-up governance. Conceding that this is happening was a hard sell to our participants even though the verdict of one of the leading thinkers about public administration,

H.G. Frederickson, would appear eminently clear: "What happened to public administration? Governance, governance everywhere" (Frederickson 2005).

Four moral contracts were presented as underpinning the corporate culture of the Canadian federal public service in order to invite precise suggestions for action on these four fronts:

- moral contract I: citizens ↔ bureaucracy;
- moral contract II: upper bureaucrats ↔ other public servants);
- moral contract III: citizens and bureaucrats at all levels ↔ politicians; and
- moral contract IV: about the style of communication (based on tact and civility) that ought to prevail among all parties. The nature of these contracts as they stand now (burdened by confrontation, distrust, anomie and incivility) seems to fit poorly with the governance requirements of the day.

Our senior executive participants were invited to reflect on what might be required in order to generate the sort of refurbishment that seems to be needed in the public service:

(i) a new 'philosophy of governance' – that fuels a continuous use of a sort of Program Review lens – recognizing the existence and importance of multiple loyalties, of wicked problems, and of the new centrality of social learning; and

(ii) a new 'philosophy of stewardship' – recognizing the importance of new competencies and the need for a refurbished human resource management system (to select, evaluate and promote people differently), for more mentoring and coaching, and for refurbished incentive reward systems.

Participants chose to focus their attention exclusively on two moral contracts: moral contract I (between citizens and the bureaucracy) and moral contract II (between the top of the bureaucracy and other public servants) – as most urgently needing to be revisited, and they chose to identify only a few blockages rather than suggesting some directions for redesign.

With respect to the first moral contract, the vertical structure and top-down mentality of the state apparatus would seem to make the kind of horizontal collaboration amongst stakeholders needed today significantly harder than it ought to be. With respect to the second moral contract, the self-censorship of risk-averse, upper bureaucrats, and the pressure from above to massage results in order to reduce controversy (making reported results odorless and colourless, and therefore stunting social learning) were seen as crucial sources of the problem.

Again there was little effort to respond to the challenges about how the transformation should be effected.

A main suggestion was to make better use of an improved Code of Values and Ethics to improve the citizen-bureaucracy moral contract, while an improved Management Accountability Framework (MAF) could help link the top of the bureaucracy to the rest of the public service. Other suggestions had to do with improved communication and efforts to increase employee engagement – and ensuring that this engagement is evaluated – *quantophrénie oblige!* – for only if it gets measured (however badly) will attention be paid to it. Finally, there was a plea for de-concentration of administrative arrangements as the way of the future – an effective effort to counter the organizational diseconomies of scale and to acknowledge that issue domains are probably the best loci of engagement. Clearly whatever might be said about these initiatives (some of which are probably useful), they are in no way attempts at redesigning the federal public service.

From leadership to stewardship

This third topic was also considered by all participants to be most difficult to tackle for it entailed nothing less than a change of paradigm: a shift from 'command and control' to an 'organic/on-going direction-finding' process, the shift from leadership to stewardship.

'Leadership' is problematic in a world where nobody is in charge, and where shared values are a myth. It reeks of hierarchy, and has mystical garb. Exceptional individuals exist, of course, who inspire colleagues and are truly charismatic leaders, but they are the exception rather than the rule. In most cases, the governance regime ensures 'stewardship': network governance to coordinate the different partners when power, resources and information are widely distributed. The least inadequate metaphor is that of an 'organic automatic pilot': an ensemble of mechanisms, always in evolution and emergence, capable of keeping the organization on track, i.e., continually adapting to the context in its social learning and direction-finding process.

To help the participants grapple with the novel concept of a stewardship process through social learning, it was presented in a simple sequential way in the form of a template used by practitioners so that suggestions for improvement might be grafted on one or the other stages more readily (Parr et al. 2002):

- Stage A begins with some perceived gap between current reality and some desirable state of affairs as a trigger to direct attention toward initiating action. There is recognition that action is required (either individually or collectively) and then an exploration of action possibilities.
- Stage B is the concurrent search for the mobilization of required partners, and the nurturing of the necessary collaboration. These dual and interactive sub-processes unfold in two steps: (1) the correct framing of critical issues and opportunities, the focussing of attention on what needs to be done, and the creation of platforms for people to work together; and (2) the communication of key information likely to inspire, rally and motivate a broader set of people to take part in the diverse networks, and the development of new relationships capable of generating tangible results, and thereby of changing mindsets and encouraging creative thinking.
- Stage C has to do with efforts to sustain change through creating and renewing institutions, and re-igniting the process by focusing again on new challenges and opportunities. This entails much conceptual

refurbishment, and efforts to agitate and rekindle the social learning process through reframing the very notion of what is possible.

What is required is a capacity for an organization to learn, i.e., to reflect on its own experience, to make sense of it, and to retool, restructure, and even to reframe the basic questions facing the organization in order to generate effective ways to grapple with the issues of concern.

These requirements have been spelled out by practitioners of reflexive governance: knowledge integration and learning by doing; capacity for long-run anticipation of systemic effects; adaptivity of strategies and institutions; iterative experimental and participatory definition of broad directions; and interactive strategy development (Voß et al. 2006).

In order for dynamic adaptation to unfold, stewardship requires competencies that need to be nudged into existence, not only by leveraging the existing forces of self-organization, but also by harnessing them to a degree. We have had occasion to mention these five categories of new competencies in the introduction (page 11). It appeared obvious through our discussions that the participants found that acquiring such competencies represented such a daunting challenge that this might explain, in part, why there was such reluctance to even accept, in principle, that such a transformation was necessary.

Indeed, in the discussion, the participants spent much time persuading themselves that such a transformation might not be necessary. Underlying this stance was the basic assumption that there must be someone in charge that kept coming back to the surface of the conversation, and remained culturally resistant to any argument to the contrary. The ideas that the context is powerful, that self-organization is very potent, and that, at best, one can nudge things a little through *bricolage* and tinkering were never really quite accepted by the participants. Accepting that things had become so complicated was deemed too complicated. Participants clung to their basic view that, in their world, capturing and wielding power is the name of the game, and that deeming it impossible was not an option.

The participants granted that power, resources and information were more widely distributed than before, and that the new game might resemble a bit more a game of GO than the old chess game. Nevertheless, much energy was spent to restate that leadership was essential, and that some elasticity for the notion of 'leadership' (relational leadership, shared leadership) would be much preferable to replacing the term with a different one (stewardship) that signaled the discontinuity clearly. The term 'leadership' would appear to serve as a security blanket.

In any case, the participants pointed out that it would be hard to bring about this kind of change calling for an expropriation of the role of top dog in a top-down system in which everything is entrenched. The current ethos of control and accountability promotes a climate of fear rather than an incentive to achieve results (Thomas 2009).

Many examples were given of officials suffering from acute cognitive dissonance with respect to the profound nature of the cultural change that would seem necessary, and indulging in a good deal of dynamic conservatism, i.e., preserving the view of the world they know at all costs despite evidence that the world is changing. Little was suggested to promote the development of this new view of the world except some executive development by the Canada School of Public Service (that used to be focused on this kind of reframing in the 1990s, a focus that has been abandoned since then) may need to be revisited.

Deputy Minister: then, now and in the future
Given the unwillingness to engage in reframing exercises revealed by the last three discussions, it is hardly surprising that the challenge of reframing or redesigning the role of deputy minister (DM) did not generate much excitement. Participants recognized that there had been a gradual drift in the nature of the task over time in the case of deputy ministers as documented in Hubbard (2009), and that, in the decades around the middle of the 20th century, senior federal officials (elected and unelected) were able to collaborate much better

than now to transform the country (Granatstein 1998). But these sorts of issues would appear beyond their world view.

Intellectually, the participants were ready to concede that the extraordinary expansion of the federal public service rendered 'informal coordination' unworkable. Scientific management became the rage and was imposed in a top-down, centralized way to try to 'control' the actions of the burgeoning public service. They also readily agreed that this led to some bad experiences as a result of the limitations of central control, and saw the beginning of the drift from Big G government to small g governance.

They also acknowledged that, starting in the late 1980s, waves of reform led by the upper, senior bureaucrats tried to bring about the necessary 'cultural change' in the federal public service, but with very limited success. The drivers of change in public management came from external developments (e.g., political, economic, social and technological) pressuring governments everywhere to adapt and adjust. Faced with this kind of profound change, senior officials have been led to gradually redefine the balance between responsiveness and loyalty on the one hand, and independence and impartiality on the other. The balancing of the burden of the DM role (in which democratic values are squarely front and centre) with personal, institutional and group interests and inclinations seems to have become more problematic.

Finally, participants acknowledged that, because of a general worldwide increase in moral relativism, groups of public servants no longer accept that they have to loyally implement legal government decisions whether or not they feel the decisions are 'not in the public interest' as defined by them. Professionalization and a guild-like mentality are becoming important for all sorts of groups, be they DMs or regulators: an emphasis on the survival and welfare of the group (i.e., the 'tribe') may even be seen as trumping democratic values at times. This is an echo of the same general phenomenon in Canadian society at large.

This being said, whatever the reasons, the participants had nothing to say about the evolving nature of the role of the DM in the future beyond the banal suggestions that there should be a need to re-emphasize the importance of selecting the right people with the right skills (e.g., change management), of better talent management (e.g., succession planning and differentiating DM jobs demanding policy skills versus those where managing is essential), of DMs being able to work horizontally (e.g., in portfolios) in ways that required collaboration rather than control, and of bringing in people from other jurisdictions or other sectors – persons who, by definition, would have a different perspective and fresh ideas.

A personal distillation of what we learned

These sessions were the end of our experiment. The topics were deliberately chosen to force the participants out of their comfort zones and, in a manner, it was probably too successful. The conversations revealed mostly what the participants would not or could not do.

Difficulty in thinking about systems

What became immensely clear in this segment of our discussions is that, despite the fact that the participants were senior executives, they were surprisingly ill-prepared to conceptualize the systems they are part of, their place in these systems and, therefore, to speculate and reflect on redesign problems or to engage meaningfully in discussions about reframing exercises. This is obviously not something that applied to all participants. A few participants were indeed able to contribute interesting ideas on this front, but their voices were drowned by the chit chat of the many who seemed to be out of their depth – not informed enough or interested enough to carry on an intelligent conversation about these issues. This was not only surprising but a major source of concern: a manifestation of the Pritchett problem we referred to earlier.

Broad perspectives would appear to frighten them. They felt comfortable only in operations and in dealing with the apparent and most obvious causes of a problem, in linear thinking which "is based on a series of logical mistakes that lead to a number of common errors when attempting to deal with complex (or wicked) problems" (Probst and Bassi 2014: 5). We came to the same conclusion when participating in executive development programs for senior executives in Ottawa. Most of them were not aware, it would seem, of this sort of flagrant deficiency – 'the failure to understand systems' – and would appear to ignore such flaws in the capabilities of senior executives and criminally re-enforce (or leave untouched) an explicit disinterest and even some hostility on the part of senior executives to being forced to engage in serious thinking about reframing and redesign.

It is not clear if this hostility is ascribable to the fact that they really think that design issues are not relevant or to the fact that they are so poorly equipped to deal with such issues that they are led to direct their attention elsewhere. In any case, this failure to understand systems would appear to be a significant weakness at the basis of their incapacity to deal effectively with design thinking. As a result, their work tends to be very myopic, geared to logistics, and responding to narrow expectations within a world where the assumption is that the problems are already well-defined and the range of alternative actions well-known. The focus is entirely on decisions about what choice should be made among well-defined alternatives. What seems to be missing is an awareness of the mental prisons haunting the present organizational culture in the Canadian federal public service cadre of senior executives.

In fact, real-life problems are not well-defined, their definitions have to be constructed, and alternatives are not well-known, they have to be discovered, created and crafted. None of this can be assumed to exist *ab ovo*. Therefore, a shift is needed from a focus on decision to a focus on design, and a course of action aimed at creating better alternatives rather than what would appear to be originally available.

Experts can't learn ...

This has been clearly explained over the last decade (Boland and Collopy 2004; Brown 2009; Paquet 2013: 82ff), but the message would not appear to have permeated the consciousness either of Canadian senior federal executives or of the specialized schools purported to train them. The reluctance of both groups to face these new challenges and to invest in developing the new, necessary skills to do this work has become a significant handicap.

The shift from a decision attitude to a design attitude that views each project "as an opportunity for invention that includes a questioning of basic assumptions and a resolve to leave the world a better place than we found it" (Boland and Collopy 2004: 9) has not been understood and therefore fully taken into account in the design of training programs for Canadian senior executives. Thus the focus on stewarding inquiring systems toward inventing assemblages of arrangements likely to foster better wayfinding and resilience – the core of modern governance – is not there, and the responses to reframing challenges could only be disappointing.

This is due in no small part to a mental block ascribable to the fact that experts are uneasy about admitting that there are things they do not know, for to so admit is tantamount to admitting that their expertise may not have been as great to begin with as they pretended. This is the Truman problem – as per the American president who denounced this mental block in his own expert entourage.

The reluctance to recognize the tectonic change from the world of Big G to the world of small g, and from a world where alternatives are already known to one where they have to be discovered and created can be easily explained by the fact that recognizing the full importance of these changes could only mean recognizing the obsolescence of much of the intellectual capital accumulated in order to deal with worlds that are now disappearing. Experts have resisted grappling with the new cosmology because the cost of doing so has appeared too high. This may explain why there has been such resistance to the invitation to define problems differently.

A tiny bit of intellectual nonchalance

Something else that may be important in explaining the incapabilities of senior executives in the face of reframing and redesigning problems is a certain intellectual nonchalance that we did not detect in our sessions with APEX but that came through and hit us between the eyes when participating in executive development programs tailored for senior executives.

In executive development programs in all fields, one finds the good, the bad and the ugly. Some of these programs are lightly disguised luxury tours, sprinkled with a few delivered papers by world experts. More common are costly programs promising useful information but not too much intellectual effort. This would appear to be the new gospel of executive education in public administration and management: entertainment and new information in pablum form are purported to suffice, on the assumption that the new reality should be easy to understand and there is no need for hard work by participants. Yet, as Thomas Pynchon reminded us, there is no reason to believe that things should be easy to understand – this raises the Pynchon problem: the complicity to trivialize executive education and to empty it of any critical thinking.

We have personally noticed that attempts to get participants to do hard work and to indulge in difficult critical thinking in many existing executive development programs for senior executives in the public sector elicits much hostility and a closing of the mind. In that sense, executive development in public administration and management has little in common with mandatory executive development in the medical, legal or other professions where continuous professional improvement is the lifeline of the profession, and executive development is an effortful investment necessary to maintain one's status in the profession. Senior executives in the public sector are not members of a profession but members of a tribe or club. Both the Truman and the Pynchon problems loom large, continuing education is not a *sine qua non*, significant and continuous intellectual capital acquisition is not *de rigueur*, and significant resistance to things that are difficult to understand can only mean failure to learn. This may be at the source of some of the learning disabilities we have witnessed.

Conclusion

A mixture of intellectual inertia and fatigue, of reluctance to go through the ordeal of paradigm shifting, of a general demise of critical thinking, of a most effective immunization against the virus of doubt, accompanied by the self-satisfaction of existing expertise, and some self-righteous hostility in the face of whatever new major intellectual effort might be required to ensure effective social learning – may prevent the slaughter of some sacred cows to proceed as it should (Paquet 2014).

References

Boland, Richard J. and Fred Collopy (eds.). 2004. *Managing by Design*. Stanford, CA: Stanford University Press.

Brown, Tim. 2009. *Change by Design*. New York, NY: Harper Business.

Frederickson, H. George. 2005. "Whatever happened to public administration? Governance, governance, everywhere|" in E. Ferlie et al. (eds.). *The Oxford Handbook of Public Management*. Oxford, UK: Oxford University Press, p. 282-304.

Granatstein, Jack L. 1998. *The Ottawa Men: The Civil Service Mandarins, 1935-1957*. Toronto, ON: University of Toronto.

Hubbard, Ruth. 2009. *Profession: Public Servant*. Ottawa, ON: Invenire Books.

Hubbard, Ruth and Gilles Paquet. 2013. "Innovation as Redesign," *www.optimumonline.ca*, 43(4): 1-13.

Paquet, Gilles. 2009. *Crippling Epistemologies and Governance Failures*. Ottawa, ON: The University of Ottawa Press.

Paquet, Gilles. 2010. "Disloyalty," *www.optimumonline.ca*, 40(1): 23-47.

Paquet, Gilles. 2013. *Tackling Wicked Policy Problems: Equality, Diversity and Sustainability*. Ottawa, ON: Invenire Books.

Paquet, Gilles. 2014. *Unusual Suspects: Essays on Social Learning Disabilities*. Ottawa, ON: Invenire Books.

Paquet, Gilles and Lise Pigeon. 2000. "In Search of a New Covenant" in E. Lindquist (ed.). *Government Restructuring and the Future of Career Public Service in Canada*. Toronto, ON: Institute of Public Administration of Canada, p. 475-498.

Parr, John et al. 2002. *The Practice of Stewardship*. Denver, CO: Alliance for Regional Stewardship.

Probst, Gilbert and Andrea Bassia. 2014. *Tackling Complexity: A Systemic Approach for Deccision Making*. Sheffield, UK: Greenleaf Publishing.

Thomas, Paul G. 2009. *Who Is Getting the Message? Communications at the Centre of Government*. Ottawa, ON: Research Study for the Oliphant Commission.

Voβ, Jan-Peter et al. (eds.). 2006. *Reflexive Governance for Sustainable Development*. Cheltenham, UK: Edward Elgar.

Annex : Basic documentation for each session

The political-bureaucratic interface

Paul G. Thomas. 2008. "Political-administrative interface in Canada's Public Sector," *www.optimumonline.ca*, 38(2): 21-29.

Federal public serviceas nexus of moral contracts

Gilles Paquet. 2009. "Gouvernance publique: (G → g) ∩ (G$_1$ → G$_2$)," *www.gouvernance.ca*, 39(4): 17-34.

Gilles Paquet. 2009. "An Agenda for Change in the Federal Public Service" in G. Paquet *Scheming virtuously: The road to collaborative governance*. Ottawa, ON: Invenire Books, chapter 8.

From leadership to stewardship

Gilles Paquet. 2009. "Stewardship Versus Leadership" in G. Paquet. *Scheming virtuously: The road to collaborative governance*. Ottawa, ON: Invenire Books, chapter 5.

Deputy Minister: then, now and in the future

Ruth Hubbard. 2009. *Profession: Public Servant*. Ottawa, ON: Invenire Books.

| Conclusion

"The number of times any of us needs to
understand systems is vanishingly small."
Lant Pritchett

There would be little sense, after conducting conversations with so many Canadian federal senior executives, in not attempting to provide some provisional conclusions of a more general nature about the state of affairs these conversations appear to have revealed. Obviously, this must be done prudently so as not to generalize unduly from the limited base of our inquiry, but it would be unconscionable not to draw attention to features that seem to characterize not only the current state of mind, but also capabilities and incapabilities of the Canadian federal senior bureaucracy, and not to propose some conjectures about what might be done to improve the situation.

Our general diagnosis may generate some contestation: many in the senior executive ranks are in denial when it comes to the pathologies of their life world. These Panglossian defenders of the present Canadian federal public administration are not friends of the federal public service, but their worst enemies. Their denials of flagrant problems can only lead to further deterioration, and perhaps ultimately to the fading away of an institution that has served Canadians well, but is, at present, in distress.

Our inquiry has had the effect of putting to the test a sample of engaged and intelligent senior executives of the Canadian federal government. While the series was designed first and foremost to meet their expressed needs, and to temper their frustrations, we could not but observe the ways in which they reacted to our pointed challenges when questions were posed to them in a relaxed and safe environment. However, attempting to read their minds and to draw conclusions from what the conversations revealed is a perilous exercise, for we cannot answer the following questions with full certitude:

- Did we succeed in making the participants feel fully at ease during these conversations?
- How frank and open did they feel they could be in these conversations?
- How revealing of their full capabilities and interests have their contributions been?
- How carefully have we listened, and have we been able to capture all the nuances of the conversations?

Being two co-animateurs with different perspectives and different sensitivities has contributed, we hope, to generating as good an environment as possible, and to reducing the possibility that we might have missed something important that was said or hinted at.

We have also been quite conscious that the difficult circumstances of the latter part of the last decade (with its mix of financial and economic difficulties, political changing of the guard, and great tensions at the political-bureaucratic interface) have created a very particular context for discussions with these senior executives. It is our view, however, that such unusual circumstances (generating more questioning than usual about the way we conduct our affairs in the public household as elsewhere) were quite propitious for this sort of inquiry. Because their world was in motion and the *status quo* was being questioned, senior executives could be expected to be particularly aware that many assumptions about the ways things had been done in the past were under scrutiny.

Therefore, it was expected that engaged senior bureaucrats would have had more opportunity and more occasions, in the intimacy of their communities of practice at work or in their homes at night, to reflect on their practice, and on what they might be willing to put forward as proposed workable re-arrangements – that is, if anyone cared to ask them their views.

Four layers of capabilities

In our APEX breakfast meetings, we proposed four series of topics for discussion to the participants. The series was intended to introduce progressively more and more difficult and demanding issues impacting on various facets of their work. This allowed us to observe and to understand their perspectives on such questions, their difficulties in dealing with them, and the sort of correctives the participants would appear to regard as desirable and feasible. The probing pertained to the following problem areas:

- How they and their colleagues coped with difficult new problems like diversity?
- How they and their colleagues were able to engage intelligently in the more demanding circumstances?
- How they and their colleagues could or wished they could interfere with processes that proved obviously flawed and administratively costly by nudging or collibrating these flawed processes? and
- How they and their colleagues would consider rewriting the rules, or redesigning the arrangements in place, in the light of the sort of reframing of perspectives that appeared to be in the process of unfolding?

Those discussions allowed us to probe the different layers of senior executives' capabilities, and to gauge their capacity to deal with these families of challenges – each one calling for some common commitment and preparation, but also requiring different intellectual abilities, as well as specific skills.

We have been very careful to allow the senior executives participating in these conversations to articulate their sentiments about these families of challenges in their own voices. What we have reported has been a mix of the difficulties that they and their colleagues have encountered in dealing with these issues, the deficiencies they were able to underline in such reactions, and the logics they evoked both in explaining why this was the case and how it was leading them to suggest some types of correctives and not others, and to assign responsibilities for such deficiencies to some sources and causes, and not others.

At the end of each chapter, we have noted some of the expressions of concern that these conversations generated, and some of the paradoxes, neuroses and the like that were evoked during the discussion period. *Seriatim* and very starkly, these were the points noted:

- decline of open critical thinking
- lack of gumption
- willful blindness in the face of mental prisons and neuroses
- incapacity and/or unwillingness to take the initiative
- impatience with contextual issues, and focus on operational details
- cognitive dissonance
- the presence of latent fear
- moral vacancy
- crippling epistemologies
- risk aversion and fear of experimentation
- failure to understand systems, and hesitation to reflect on their redesign
- reluctance to admit that experts must learn
- disinterest in the face of new perspectives difficult to understand

This list in no way does justice to the careful arguments in support of these sources of *malaise*, but it amounts to a sort of indictment of the community of Canadian federal senior executives as echoed by a sample of intelligent and particularly engaged participants. It might be regarded as a fair view of the state of mind of the tribe of these senior executives. Moreover, as we explained earlier in the text (chapters 1 through 4), the concerns seemed to be growing more and more severe as we proceeded from chapter 1 to chapter 4, i.e., as one proceeds from probing the different capacities to cope, to engage, to collibrate and to reframe. It was expected that this situation would lead naturally to more and more radical suggestions for correctives as we proceeded to the latter phases, but this was not the case. As the issues became more difficult to handle, there was also a sense that our sample of senior executives became somewhat overwhelmed by the immensity of the task, and therefore less inclined to allow themselves to speculate on what might be done to correct the situation. Whether this reluctance to come forward with suggestions was the result of some lack of preparedness or capacity to tackle such problems, or the result of a choice not to engage in such reflections because they were considered out of bounds, was not always clear.

Most certainly, as the issues became less easily handled by routine mechanical repairs, or broad generalities about the directions in which one should proceed, the participants became less talkative, and less and less willing to allow their imaginations to play an exploratory role. Indeed, one could see a preference for bringing the discussion back to a marginal technical dimension to avoid entering the dangerous world of design.

A syndrome ... tentatively

Our tentative diagnosis is presented in five steps.

First, it is clear that the Canadian federal public service has become immense and more complex over the last few decades. Our more globalized and pluralistic world has experienced accelerated change, and posed ever more wicked problems to decision makers as it becomes clear that nobody is fully in charge, that the public domain is being transformed and somewhat contained, and that the false impression of a secure Gaussian view of the world (with tamed variance) has to be replaced with a view of the "world that is immensely more chaotic." Clearly, a significant portion of the difficulties experienced by Canadian public governance is ascribable to this transformation of the environment – a matter beyond its control, but one that it has had to acknowledge, to keep in mind, and to confront. It has generated challenges that have not been handled by the senior executives as well as might have been expected (Paquet 1999a, 2005, 2013a).

Second, it is also clear that one of the main reasons why good governance has not been achieved – i.e., effective coordination when resources, power and resources are widely distributed, and nobody from the private, public, or social sectors is fully in charge – is the hysteresis of the Canadian system: its memory, its path-dependence, its 'baggage' of mental prisons carried over from another era. An antiquated system of beliefs (the dogma that someone must always be in charge, the necessity of centralization, state centricity as a must, the belief in mythical Canadian values, the fixation on egalitarianism, etc.) has remained vibrant in the Canadian federal public service, and too many of the senior executives continue to see their role as guardians of those mythical values. The pursuit and defence of these beliefs would appear to have blinded the senior Canadian public service to the challenges of global realities and to the imperatives imposed by them. Crippling epistemologies, learned blindness, fear of experimentation and the like have taken their toll (Paquet 2009).

Third, the senior executives have been torn between the mental prisons inherited from the past (sometimes the recent past), and the new imperatives imposed by the present context. These tensions, and the ensuing governance failures, have traumatized the state and its officers. Old techniques have failed, public confidence has declined, deference has disappeared, and learned helplessness has invaded the world of public administration. This has led to denial, risk aversion, and fear of experimentation. Neuroses have surfaced everywhere, and fictions have been invented in a futile effort to exorcize the new chaotic world. In our view, the state of mind of senior federal executives has come to be tainted by a multitude of bad habits: creeping cognitive dissonance and political correctness, erosion of critical thinking, etc. These bad habits of the mind have unwittingly led to reprehensible behaviour: rewarding failure, punishing success, failure to confront, disloyalty, etc. Various forms of organizational violence ensued. Much of the material in this volume has documented this state of affairs. A synthetic version of this diagnosis as it pertains to Canadian society at large may be found in Higham and Paquet (2013).

Fourth, these blockages could not but generate systemic failures and pathologies of governance at the very time that senior federal executives appear to have developed an inability to engage in systems thinking, or even to appreciate that this was an important inadequacy. A growing dynamic conservatism, a decline in the capacity to transform and to learn, deepening symptoms of neuroses, and consequent efforts to rationalize one's own incapacities and inertia, etc. – these are all features that we have documented earlier (Hubbard and Paquet 2007, 2010).

Fifth, in the face of these various pressures and toxicities, the Canadian senior public service executives might have been able to develop effective strategies if they had been able to crystallize into a 'community of practice' – an organizational form capable of developing an integrative way of dealing with the various facets of wicked policy problems. However, instead of developing in this direction, the Canadian federal public service has instead degenerated into squabbles with a string of unions, tribes and clubs operating in siloed domains. This approach has proven unable to generate a systems perspective, and consequently, has not been able to evolve the necessary basic fail-safe and safe-fail mechanisms capable of ensuring both the integrity and the resilience of the public service stewardship system, nor to guide the emergence of the capacities and potentialities for the socio-economy to transform, innovate and progress (Brown et al. 2010; Hubbard et al. 2012).

Starkly summarizing these points in bringing this book to a close may generate a sense of inexorability and hopelessness. This is neither our view nor our goal. The key objective is to bring these trends into visibility, to question the adequacy of the existing mindset and capabilities of the cadre of senior executives, and to suggest that the Canadian federal public service is facing critical times and needs to transform.

Cosmology-less wayfinding

These various forces, blockages and pathologies have resulted mainly from the misfits between the ever more complex and wicked challenges and the inadequacies of the administrative apparatuses invented to deal with them. As early as the 1990s, there was evidence of the inadequacy of the traditional cosmology which prevailed in the federal public service despite the challenges generated by the new realities of network governance and small g governance (Paquet 1999b); and there was some evidence that much of the effort to create a useful response was foundering on the immense fragmentation and incoherence of the federal human resources regime. This has resulted in two decades of improvisation without the guidance of any integrative cosmology (Lindquist and Paquet 2000).

There was an enormous chasm between the task to be performed and the human resource arrangements concatenated by the various heads of the multiple agencies supposedly in charge of one segment or another of the federal human resources 'regime': a sort of Hydra that seemed to grow two heads for each one that was cut off, and would have required Hercules' firebrand to ensure its slaying and its replacement by an integrative entity that would reconnect this regime with some sort of performance imperative. But there was no Hercules in sight, and no new cosmology has crystallized. What has materialized has been a variety of uncoordinated *ad hoc* initiatives hooked up to different horses pulling the human resources cart in its own idiosyncratic direction.

The various toxic forces mentioned above strained not only the human resources regime, but all the crucial interfaces in the federal public administration process (among the citizens, the politicians, the bureaucrats, the different sectors, and the different levels of government) as a result of the lack of an integrative view. Collaborative governance may have been the new categorical imperative, but the Canadian federal senior executives appear to have been ill-prepared for their role as *animateurs* and designers in this collaborative governance world. Even though, at a certain level of generality, some senior executives perceived that this crucial role was theirs to play, that it was part of their burden of office, they seemed not up to the task or else to regard such tasks as not part of their burden of office: the former having often generated the latter.

If through our conversations with this group of engaged and interested Canadian senior federal executives our review has captured fairly the state of the bureaucratic mind, and has gauged fairly the capabilities of the senior bureaucracy, then it was clear that more and more inadequacies became apparent as the conversations went on:

- the group seemed at first to find it difficult to cope with some of the big contextual challenges;
- it had much more difficulty in engaging intelligently and in a fully satisfactory way with the crucial tasks of collective governing of the public household; yet it appeared to struggle honourably to meet these more complex and yet relatively routine tasks;
- significant inadequacy was revealed in the collibration work; and
- the group seemed thoroughly unprepared for their reframing and organizational redesign work.

This carefully-worded if provocative diagnosis, built on an accumulation of facts, reactions, impressions and apprehensions, is presented as nothing more than an 'action hypothesis' *à la* Friedmann-Abonyi. As such, it needs to be handled somewhat differently than usual hypotheses.

Traditional approaches to policy research focus on attempts to falsify hypotheses about some objective reality, according to the canons of scientific experimentation. This is too narrow a focus for policy research and action hypotheses in turbulent times. For the social practitioner, what is central is an effort "to create a wholly new, unprecedented situation that, in its possibility for generating new knowledge, goes substantially beyond the initial hypothesis" (Friedmann and Abonyi 1976: 936). The social learning paradigm is built on reflection-in-action, dialogue and mutual learning by experts and clients.

"The paradigm makes the important epistemological assumption that action hypotheses are verified as 'correct' knowledge only in the course of a social practice that includes the four components of theory (of reality), the configuration of values, strategy and action. A further epistemological commitment is to the creation of a new reality, and hence to a new knowledge, rather than in establishing the truth-value of propositions in abstraction from the social context to which they are applied" (*Ibid.*: 938).

To deal with wicked problems, analysts must learn on the job about both the configuration of facts and values defining the issues. They must also learn from the stakeholders, as well as from the megacommunity. Without their participation (active and passive), it is unlikely that a collaborative governance apparatus can be distilled that will synthesize, reconcile and transcend the perspectives of the different potential partners, nor can an effective and sustained collaboration be generated among those who hold a portion of the power, resources and information required to ensure effective wayfinding, resilience and innovation.

Some decades ago, Friedmann and Abonyi stylized a simple social learning model of policy research to deal with wicked problems. They have suggested that it requires responding to four questions about any possible action plan: Is it technically feasible? Is it socially acceptable? Is it too politically destabilizing? Is it implementable? In order to respond to these questions, it requires some appreciation (1) of appropriate theories of reality, (2) of the ways social values are expressed, (3) of the political game within which the design exercise is carried out, and (4) of the ways in which collective action is carried out. These four pillars of social learning are interconnected, and any change in one affects the others. This paradigm of social practice in policy research is synthesized here.

A Social Learning Model of Policy Research

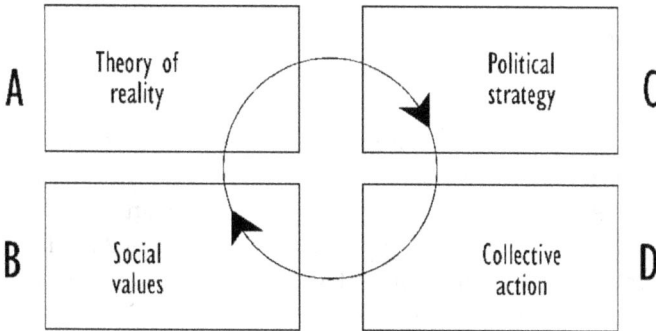

Source: Friedman and Abonyi, 1976, p. 934.

This is the sort of apparatus required to comprehensively explore the scene of wicked problems. This is also the sort of framework that senior executives need to use in order to approach the sort of challenges they face in our modern socio-economies: searching for responses that are technically feasible, socially acceptable, not too politically destabilizing, and implementable with the help of partners. But this broad exploratory framework cannot suffice. It can only serve as a foundation on which to build a new inquiring system likely to throw light on the sort of regime or covenants that will bring forth the new capabilities the federal senior executives of the Canadian government need to be able to do their jobs better.

The way out and forward ... a catwalk

A catwalk is defined as a narrow walkway affording passage over and around areas not otherwise traversable, or giving access to places otherwise inaccessible.

To the extent that our appraisal of the state of affairs is reasonable, a number of correctives are clearly required. New capacities must be developed at the four levels we have probed all along – cognitive, behavioural, organizational and institutional – in order to break down the stubborn resistance to change at each of these levels. To fix ideas, we suggest that this work must manage to fill in three families of gaps at each of these levels: governance gaps at the level of knowledge, norms and mechanisms.

Our intent is not to provide a comprehensive list of all the actions called for in each of these 12 cells, but only to put forward a provisional list of initiatives designed to kick start the necessary conversation about what the catwalk might entail. At a time in January 2014 when the Canadian federal government had announced that it intends to overhaul many aspects of the organization of work for the senior executives (May 2014), it may serve as a reminder that such overhauling cannot be significantly value-adding if it remains at the level of dusting off the EX categories and repackaging them. What is required is a rethinking of the capacities and capabilities of senior executives in our complex and uncertain world plagued with wicked problems.

Cognitively speaking, this means remedying the lack of systems thinking, of wider perspectives and longer time horizons, and of appreciation for learning by doing (Paquet 2012). This more holistic approach would call for rethinking the norms in the direction of more critical thinking, an appreciation of ecological rationality, and adherence to a post-positivist perspective that puts in question the scientistic posture in good currency. This calls for new mechanisms that lead to a systematic questioning of the assumptions in good currency, and ways to generate new, broader perspective points (as one would expect from elevated views from a crane). This can only emerge from a significant rethinking of the executive education in public administration (Normann 2001; Pritchett 2013).

Behaviourally speaking, what is called for is a greater willingness of senior executives to get out of their zones of comfort and nonchalance, and to work harder at understanding what is not familiar, to cease thinking only linearly, and to have the courage to expose deceit. This entails redefining the burden of office: learning as the imperative, frankness as inescapable, and commitment as a *sine qua non*, a renaissance of experimentation and of design thinking activities, and the restoration of the sort of pride, professionalism and the code of honour that used to be in good currency in the public sector elite, and that has been immensely eroded over the past few decades (Sabel 2001; Cuisinier 2008; Appiah 2010). The redefined burden of office for senior public officials would drift away from the narrow focus on technical decisions within a static framework (where the problem is already defined, and the possible alternatives well known), toward a recognition that the problem definition has to be constructed, that possible alternatives have to be created and crafted, and that this entails constructing inquiring systems and designing organizations (Boland and Collopy 2004; Paquet and Wilson 2011).

Agenda for Capacities Refurbishment to Fill the Gaps

| | GAPS | | |
	Knowledge	Norms	Mechanisms
CAPACITIES			
Cognitive	systems thinking	thinking critically	question assumptions
	exploration	ecological rationality	view from a crane
	delta knowledge	post-positivist	rethink education
Behavioural	effort to understand	learning as main goal	experimentation
	lateral thinking	calling a spade a spade	design thinking
	exposing deceit	*affectio societatis*	code of honour
Organizational	identify mental prisons	moral contracts	agoras for dialogue
	expose the idol of the tribe	seeking antifragility	forbidding fear
Institutional	context	performance	fail-safe
		quality control	safe-fail

Organizationally speaking, it entails recognizing the invidious presence of mental prisons and neuroses, and the toxic loyalty of senior executives to the bureaucratic tribe – something that cripples their work and leads to blindness in the face of ignominious acts by colleagues. This calls for new norms of antifragility: to replace the existing built-in incentive reward system and the moral contracts that discourage experimentation with alternative arrangements that foster collective learning and make uncertainty, complexity and avalanches into triggers for accelerated learning and greater innovative intensity (Duhigg 2012; Taleb 2012; Paquet 2013b).

Institutionally speaking, the focus should be on the power of context, on the core importance of performance and quality control at the norms level, and on the development of mechanisms to ensure resilience (fail-safe) in normal times, and a dramatic transformation (safe-fail) when the institution is faced with dramatic forms of creative destruction (Hubbard et al. 2012: 85-86). To develop the capabilities to face the latter sort of challenges, collaborative governance is necessary. This, in turn, requires the emergence of communities of practice and the renaissance of a new epistemology of practice (Friedmann 1978) that would underpin the development, maintenance and continuous enhancement of something like a paradigm of open collective transdisciplinary and imagination-fuelled inquiry (Brown et al. 2010: 294).

One can see the immensity of the renewal that these drifts will require in the knowledge base, in the norms, and in the array of mechanisms in use, thereby filling in the ominous gaps that have been identified in the course of our conversations with these senior executives.

Toward a new covenant through a new inquiring system

Whether or not this catwalk will sound appealing, the problems to be resolved for Canadian senior executives in the public service will not disappear, despite the fact that too many of the *principaux intéressés* remain in denial. It is unlikely that the senior executives' present state of incapacities will remain unnoticed, despite the uncritical and senseless exhortation by so many academics for whom our senior public sector executives are knights to whom we should turn to save us from the political knaves who are running the public household so badly. This sort of mindless celebration of managerialism by academics (both as an ideology and as a preferred way of governing) has bolstered blindness to the grievous flaws of the bureaucracy that our conversations with senior executives have revealed.

The issue is not a matter of blaming the bureaucrats for everything that goes wrong, but of noting that the bureaucracy is not immune to sins of commission and omission, and that there is a real danger when academics continue to refer to them with a certain degree of unctuousness as a clergy with a special calling (Kernaghan 2007). Indeed, even super-bureaucrats like the Auditor General or the Parliamentary Budget Officer have been unconscionable in allowing their denunciations to be interpreted as an attack on the politicians, when many of the exactions they unearthed are the deeds of bureaucrats. An unhealthy protective belt appears to surround senior executives. There is a great insouciance in gauging their performance, and a glaring neglect on their part to live up to the requirements of their burden of office and to honour their moral contracts. The response to these failings is not more rigidity and controls, but a renaissance from within. Our probing of the bureaucratic mindset and its failings is a first step on the way to a catharsis.

If, as we suggest, the Canadian federal senior executives are more and more often faced with wicked problems that they are seemingly ill-prepared to tackle, it would be naïve to believe that a useful response to this nexus of difficulties can be elicited without an improved and more sophisticated inquiring system in use that can match the complexity of the issue itself.

At the end of the 1990s, Paquet and Pigeon (2000) proposed (on the basis of some conversations with participants in courses at the Canadian Centre for Management Development – now the Canada School of Public Service) the contours of a new covenant that would redefine the work of the senior public service. The most generous way to define the reaction to this blueprint is that it was not well-received.

That work may have been premature. The deep crisis of the public service was only then emerging, and was not widely regarded as being as lethal as it would later prove to be. It was also right after the fiascos of both the Nielsen Task Force in the 1980s and of PS 2000 in the 1990s, in the euphoria of renewed economic growth of the late 1990s (after the 1995 radical action to deal with the fiscal crisis) and under the spell of the hangover of the 1995 referendum on Quebec secession. The mind of the federal government was not on what were still considered at the time as 'housekeeping' issues, and that were only to be recognized, in fact, as matters of governance later on. It may also be that a language of moral contracts was used in our defining of the new covenant – a language that was perhaps impossible to understand at the time. More importantly, this covenant was offered from critical quarters outside the confines of the tribe. No such offering could ever have been regarded as legitimate.

Since the lessons of the last 30 years have persuasively established that a legitimate new covenant defining the burden of office and the required capabilities for senior bureaucrats is most unlikely to come from within the tribe, and that it is also most unlikely to be acceptable as an offering from their critics, the best bet would appear to be a roundabout process that would start with a refurbished mental toolbox and a piecemeal and collaborative approach that would escape those blind alleys.

The Australian experience may be interesting in this context. It would appear to be too straightforward and practical to be acceptable in the Canadian context, yet it holds some lessons as to the sort of process that can lead to the refurbishment that is regarded as necessary.

It began with the Australian Public Service Commission (2007) producing a briefing paper applying the Rittel and Webber (1973) wicked problem approach to national policy fields. This was an eye-opening experiment.

First, it brought the characteristics of wicked problems, identified by Rittel and Webber, into visibility in national debates:

- multiple interpretations with no one version right or wrong;
- interdependencies involving multiple causality and trade-offs between conflicting goals;
- addressing the problem leading to unforeseen consequences;
- problem definition not stable but a moving target;
- no definitive solution;
- great social complexity;
- rarely tractable within one discipline, or organization, so difficult to position responsibility; and
- resolution involving personal and social behavioural changes.

Second, it also revealed that such wicked problems cannot be generalized outside their contexts, that they rest on underlying paradoxes (self-contradictory statements in which both propositions are true), and that they contain multiple world views, multiple ways of constructing knowledge, multiple ethical positions. In a word, it requires a different sort of inquiring system, much different from the standard linear approaches in good currency in public administration (Brown et al. 2010: 62-64).

Third, in part as an echo effect of this initiative by the Australian Public Service Commission, a research team at the Australian National University got involved in developing guiding principles for an open, critical, transdisciplinary, collective and imagination-fuelled systemic approach to dealing with wicked policy problems. While their interest was largely focused on sustainability, it has put in place the foundations of a broader approach capable of tackling wicked policy problems of all sorts. This approach has been summarized synthetically by Jacqueline Y. Russell (2010: 56-58) as anchored in:

- the partiality, plurality and provisionality of knowing;
- the reliability of knowledge being gauged by critical and intersubjective assessment;

- the awareness of the purposes, agendas and values on the inquiring process;
- including both facts and values in the inquiry process; and
- openness to the ontological, epistemological and ethical rationalities.

It has been suggested that the sort of inquiring system required is to proceed in four stages (Brown et al. 2010: 78):

1. identify the range of world views that make up the context of the problem;
2. establish the validity of the evidence that each of the knowledges can provide;
3. create the conditions that sponsor creativity among the diverse participants; and
4. develop a strategy that allows all the contributing knowledges to share possible actions for the future.

This may appear to be rather sketchy, but it proposes a genuinely unconventional and innovative approach that has been able to generate illuminating results in a large number of case studies (*Ibid.*: Part II), and that later has been stylized in the form of a textbook that shows the way, step by step, to design collective learning for transformational change (Brown and Lambert 2013).

Such an approach – open to different world views, transdisciplinary, critical, collective and allowing imagination to play its role in the design of future arrangements – would appear to pave the way for the development of a more comprehensive approach to the challenges they face, and to suggest the contours of a new covenant for senior executives in the public service if they are to meet the Friedmann-Abonyi test: guided by the need to establish that their initiatives are technically feasible, socially acceptable, not too destabilizing, and implementable to begin with.

A social learning approach, built on cognate intentions, has been developed in parallel at the Centre on Governance at the University of Ottawa. It has also been applied to wicked policy problems of all sorts on the broad public administration scene over the years (Paquet 1999a, 2013b). But it has never met any interest in Canada on the part of the public administration community. We were told that it was difficult to understand. What is clear is that the stimulus for change must come from outside the public administration tribe, but from a position that has some 'skin in the game' – the game being necessarily broader than the field of interest of the federal senior executives alone.

It is, therefore, unlikely that a venture such as the one that was kick-started by the Australian Public Service Commission would be considered in Canada. Thus, a more oblique form of attack on the incapabilities of senior executives needs to be envisaged, one that at first blush would not appear to require the development of such a new *outillage mental*. In Canada, critical thinking is not our cup of tea in this issue domain: obliquity is *de rigueur* (Kay 2010).

Were it not that the Senate of Canada has suffered much damage recently at the hands of a plague of rogues, allowing one of its committees to investigate the Canadian public governance system and the way to ensure the refurbishment of the cadre of Canadian public service senior executives would appear to be an interesting option. It has proved to be a most useful device in dealing with complex issues like aging, poverty, science policy, and the thorny issue of health care.

Perhaps what is needed is something that will sound more pragmatic and in the nature of a short-term device. This will only allow new perspectives to be shepherded in as the experience unfolds. Whatever innocuous move might trigger the search for a new covenant, it should be clear that it is not going to be the result of a deliberate effort to reframe the perspectives – this is not the Canadian way! Rather, it will have to start with a simple practical move that will only later allow the development of an emergent strategy, emanating from the more or less clumsy efforts mediated and transformed by the power of context and by unforeseen consequences ascribable to an environment no one really controls (Martin 2014).

One starting point

Such a move might take the form of the creation of a federal Ministry of the Public Service to put some order into the Canadian federal public service. It would have as an explicit mandate to explore the realities behind the myth of the public service as a lump of homogeneous labour (Hubbard and Paquet 2010: chapter 10) and to come forward with a new partitioning of the public service in order to make it more innovative and effective in the face of the challenges created by the small g governance world. A junior but forceful and widely respected minister to the Treasury Board could (within the federal government's financial constraints) be asked to design a better way to govern this country, and to redesign the Canadian federal public service to make the highest and best use of its varied human resources. This would undoubtedly lead to the development of a new set of perspectives, and to the construction of new covenants, but only as an unintended consequence – something that could not be anticipated and therefore could not be stopped.

The drift from top-down Big G government to a more inclusive and horizontal small g governance (as a result of the growing turbulence of the environment, and of the greater variety and complexity of the socio-economic systems to be governed when no one is in charge) has transformed the governing process: more stakeholders with different interests and competencies have come to be involved in the stewardship of the socio-economy. A few 'intelligent generalists' (however imaginative or competent) can no longer as easily 'scheme virtuously' and have a huge impact on policy choices and/ or ensure successful execution. The world is so complex, and there are so many players. Ashby's law applies. Variety in the regulator has to increase because of the greater variety in the system being regulated.

As a result, new units of management analysis (e.g., regions, categories of workers, issue domains) are of the essence, as well as new units of policy analysis (e.g., city-regions, communities of practice). On the human resource

(HR) management front, many different categories of public sector workers have crystallized, and have received more or less formal recognition through unions or categories of types of employment. Central agencies and management boards of all sorts must take notice of this new context, and change their perspectives accordingly: top-down, one-size-fits-all mechanisms will no longer work. Central agencies will have to allow for enough flexibility in organizational arrangements and work environments (e.g., work structure and work systems, procurement, administration, finance, IT, etc.), while focusing on the ligatures that will be needed to knit together the quilt of organizational and institutional arrangements that have sprung to life (different institutional ecologies) into relatively coherent wholes in the name of efficiency, effectiveness, fairness and legitimacy.

The partitioning of the public service as set out in the figure on page 136 might be a prototype worth putting on the table to start the conversation. It provides a rough picture of the coverage and size of four categories of public servants, but also of the burden of office of members of these different categories, and of the citizens' legitimate expectations about their work. This type of partitioning constitutes a powerful argument against a one-size-fits-all approach: public sector employment identifies different types of burden of office, requiring different types of human capital, and employment relations and regimes.

Group 1 represents core human capital, both highly unique and valuable. They are at the inner core, and their employment relationships tend to be long term and focused on organizational commitment and trust. Group 2 represents human capital that is highly valuable, but less unique. The employment relationship will tend to be relatively more focused on immediate performance and a results-based approach. Group 3 represents idiosyncratic human capital that has specialized knowledge, and is not always easy to find in the market, but is readily available most of the time; it requires an employment relationship that is based on a partnership that preserves some continuity over time. Group 4 may be regarded as ancillary human capital that is of less strategic value and not unique to the organization; the focus there is more on compliance with pre-set rules, regulations and procedures.

Human Capital in Canadian Public Service[9]

Higher ↑	3) Professionals	1) Super-bureaucrats
	Main challenge: Balance professional & political Main job: Ideas, innovation & horizontality HR goal: Learning (40.000)	Burden of office: Safeguard fabric of society Main job: Co-governing & enabling HR goal: Commitment (< 500)
	4) Employees	2) Guardians
Uniqueness	Main challenge: Reliability & fairness Main job: Productivity HR goal: Responsiveness (185,000)	Burden of office: Loyalty Main job: Management HR goal: Productivity (<10,000)

Value Higher ⟶

We do not propose this partitioning as a magic bullet to heal all the ills of the Canadian federal public service or to cure all the foibles observed at the senior executive levels. But we do believe the sort of conversations that would be triggered by the discussion of such a scheme to be a useful prototype – something provisional that can probably be improved upon but might also serve as a basis for deliberation – and powerful enabler of the necessary renewal.

[9] Adapted from Morris et al. 2005. The size of the federal public service was estimated at about 235,000 (including separate agencies like Revenue Canada) in 2007.

In summary

Cynics might suggest that such an innocuous nudge would generate no impact at all. This is not our view. Such a seemingly strict administrative and operational move would entail, of necessity, the emergence of larger perspectives in the conversation that will follow, and the development of an inquiring system that is going to be much more encompassing of different world views than would have been regarded as palatable in the Canadian context if this had been proposed right off the bat.

This initiative would not provide a definitive answer to a problem conclusively defined, but only the beginning of a conversation about what the new public service might look like – one dedicated "to help citizens articulate and meet their shared interests rather than attempt to control and steer society" (Denhardt and Vinzant Denhardt 2000).

It also might help a great deal in pressing forward the sort of agenda defined by Kevin Lynch (the then Clerk of the Privy Council and Head of the Canadian Public Service) in a speech to members of APEX at its 2006 annual symposium. At the time, he singled out five areas of focus for the Canadian federal public service: a) clarity around roles, responsibilities and accountabilities; b) teamwork; c) the quest for excellence; d) matching people with work and meeting the renewal challenges; and e) the capacity to think about the future (facing the wicked policy challenges).

The discussions around a new partitioning of the federal public service would allow new potentialities to blossom, new forms of complementarities and collaboration to emerge, and prototypes of new covenants for senior public sector executives to be discussed. The magic of dialogue will do the rest (Yankelovich 1999).

References

Appiah, K. Anthony. 2010. *The Honor Code – How Moral Revolutions Happen*. New York, NY: Norton.

Boland, Richard J. and Fred Collopy. 2004. *Managing by Design*. Stanford, CA: Stanford University Press.

Brown, Valerie A. et al. (eds.). 2010. *Tackling Wicked Problems – Through Transdisciplinary Imagination*. London, UK: Earthscan.

Brown, Valerie A. and Judith A. Lambert. 2013. *Collective Learning for Transformational Change – A Guide to Collaborative Action*. London, UK: Routledge.

Cuisinier, Vincent. 2008. *L'affectio societatis*. Paris, FR: Lexis-Nexis Litec.

Denhardt, Robert B. and Janet Vinzant Denhardt. 2000. "The New Public Service: Serving rather than Steering," *Public Administration Review*, 60(6): 549-559.

Duhigg, Charles. 2012. *The Power of Habit – Why we do what we do in life and business*. Toronto, ON: Doubleday.

Friedmann, John. 1978. "The Epistemology of Social Practice," *Theory and Society*, 6(1): 75-92.

Friedmann, John and George Abonyi. 1976. "Social Learning: A Model for Policy Research," *Environment & Planning*, A8, p. 927-940.

Higham, Robin and Gilles Paquet. 2013. "Reflections on the Canadian Malaise," *www.optimumonline.ca*, 43(2): 1-12.

Hubbard, Ruth and Gilles Paquet. 2007. *Gomery's Blinders and Canadian Federalism*. Ottawa, ON: The University of Ottawa Press.

Hubbard, Ruth and Gilles Paquet. 2010. *The Black Hole of Public Administration*. Ottawa, ON: The University of Ottawa Press.

Hubbard, Ruth et al. 2012. *Stewardship – Collaborative Decentred Metagovernance and Inquiring Systems*. Ottawa, ON: Invenire Books.

Kay, John. 2010. *Obliquity – Why our goals are best achieved indirectly*. London, UK: The Penguin Press.

Kernaghan, Kenneth. 2007. *A Special Calling: Values, Ethics, and Professional Public Service*. Ottawa, ON: Canada Public Service Agency.

Lindquist, Evert and Gilles Paquet. 2000. "Government Restructuring and the Federal Public Service – The Search for a New Cosmology" in E. Lindquist (ed.). *Government Restructuring and Career Public Services*. Toronto, ON: IPAC, p. 71-111.

Martin, Roger L. 2014. "The Big Lie of Strategic Planning," *Harvard Business Review*, 92(1-2): 79-84.

May, Kathryn. 2014. "Review targets public sector executives," *Ottawa Citizen*, January 13.

Morris, Shad S. et al. 2005. "An Architectural Approach to Managing Knowledge Stocks and Flows: Implications for Reinventing the HR Function," Working Paper Series. Ithica, NY: Cornell University, School of Industrial and Labour Relations, Center for Advanced Human Resource Studies.

Normann, Richard. 2001. *Reframing Business*. Chichester, UK: Wiley.

Paquet, Gilles. 1999a. "Tackling Wicked Problems" in G. Paquet, *Governance Through Social Learning*. Ottawa, ON: The University of Ottawa Press, chapter 2.

Paquet, Gilles. 1999b. "Innovations in Governance in Canada," *Optimum*, 29(2-3): 71-81.

Paquet, Gilles. 1999c. *Governance through Social Learning*. Ottawa, ON: The University of Ottawa Press.

Paquet, Gilles. 2005. *The New Geo-Governance – A Baroque Approach*. Ottawa, ON: The University of Ottawa Press.

Paquet, Gilles. 2009. *Crippling Epistemologies and Governance Failures – A Plea for Experimentalism*. Ottawa, ON: The University of Ottawa Press.

Paquet, Gilles. 2012. "La gouvernance, science de l'imprécis," *Organisations & Territoires*, 21(3): 5-17.

Paquet, Gilles. 2013a. "The Political-Bureaucratic Interface: a comment on Andrew Griffith's expedition," *www.optimumonline.ca*, 43(4): 61- 74.

Paquet, Gilles. 2013b. *Tackling Wicked Policy Problems: Equality, Diversity and Sustainability*. Ottawa, ON: Invenire.

Paquet, Gilles and Lise Pigeon. 2000. "In Search of a New Covenant" in E. Lindquist (ed.). *Government Restructuring and Career Public Services*. Toronto, ON: IPAC, p. 475-498.

Paquet, Gilles and Christopher Wilson. 2011. "Collaborative Co-governance and Inquiring Systems," *www.optimumonline.ca*, 41(2): 1-12.

Pritchett, Lant. 2013. *The Rebirth of Education – Schooling ain't Learning*. Washington, DC: Brookings Institution.

Rittel, H and M. Webber. 1973. "Dilemmas in a General Theory of Planning," *Policy Sciences*, 4, p. 155-169.

Russell, Jacqueline Y. 2010. "A Philosohical Framework for an Open and Critical Transdisciplinary Inquiry" in Brown, Valerie A. et al. (eds.). *Tackling Wicked Problems – Through Transdisciplinary Imagination*. London, UK: Earthscan, p. 31-60.

Sabel, Charles F. 2001. "A Quiet Revolution of Democratic Governance: Towards Democratic Experimentalism" in *Governance in the 21st Century*. Paris, FR: OECD, p. 121-148.

Taleb, Nassim N. 2012. *Antifragile – Things that gain from disorder*. New York, NY: Random House.

Yankelovich, Daniel. 1999. *The Magic of Dialogue – Transforming Conflict into Cooperation*. New York, NY: Simon & Schuster.

| References

The material in chapters 1 to 4 has been published in a slightly different form in the following papers:

Hubbard, Ruth and Gilles Paquet. 2007. "Cat's Cradling: APEX Forum on Wicked Problems," *www.optimumonline.ca*, 37(2): 12-18.

Hubbard, Ruth and Gilles Paquet. 2008. "Cat's Eyes: Intelligent Work Versus Perverse Incentives – APEX Forum on Wicked Problems ," *www.optimumonline.ca*, 38(3): 1-22.

Hubbard, Ruth and Gilles Paquet. 2009. "Not in the catbird seat: Pathologies of governance," *www.optimumonline.ca*, 39(2): 11-20.

Hubbard, Ruth and Gilles Paquet. 2009. "The Unwisdom of Cats," *www.optimumonline.ca*, 39(4): 52-66.

Titles in the Collaborative Decentred Metagovernance Series

6. Ruth Hubbard and Gilles Paquet   2014
   Probing the Bureaucratic Mind:
   About Canadian Federal Executives

5. Gilles Paquet   2013
   Gouvernance corporative : une entrée en matières

4. Gilles Paquet   2013
   Tackling Wicked Policy Problems:
   Equality, Diversity and Sustainability

3. Gilles Paquet and Tim Ragan   2012
   Through the Detox Prism: Exploring Organizational
   Failures and Design Responses

2. Gilles Paquet   2012
   Moderato cantabile: Toward Principled Governance
   for Canada's Immigration Policy

1. Ruth Hubbard, Gilles Paquet and
   Christopher Wilson   2012
   Stewardship: Collaborative Decentred Metagovernance
   and Inquiring Systems

Other titles published by INVENIRE

16. Marc Gervais   2012
    Challenges of Minority Governments in Canada

15. Caroline Andrew, Ruth Hubbard
    et Gilles Paquet (sld.)   2012
    Gouvernance communautaire :
    innovations dans le Canada français hors Québec

14. Tom Brzustowski   2012
    Why we need more Innovation in Canada and
    what we must do to get it

13. Claude M. Rocan   2012
    Challenges in Public Health Governance:
    The Canadian Experience

12. Richard Clément et Caroline Andrew (sld.)   2012
    Villes et langues : gouvernance et politiques
    Symposium international

11. Richard Clément and Caroline Andrew (eds.)   2012
    Cities and Languages: Governance and Policy
    International Symposium

10. Michael Behiels and François Rocher (eds.)   2011
    The State in Transition: Challenges for
    Canadian Federalism

9. Pierre Camu   2011
    La Flotte Blanche : Histoire de la Compagnie de
    Navigation du Richelieu et d'Ontario, 1845-1913

8. Rupak Chattopadhyay and Gilles Paquet (eds.)   2011
    The Unimagined Canadian Capital:
    Challenges for the Federal Capital Region

7. Gilles Paquet   2011
    Tableau d'avancement II : Essais exploratoires sur la
    gouvernance d'un certain Canada français

6. James Bowen (ed.)   2011
    The Entrepreneurial Effect: Waterloo

5. François Lapointe   2011
    Cities as Crucibles: Reflections on Canada's
    Urban Future

4. James Bowen (ed.)   2009
    The Entrepreneurial Effect

3. Gilles Paquet   2009
    Scheming virtuously: the road to collaborative governance

2. Ruth Hubbard   2009
    Profession: Public Servant

1. Robin Higham   2009
    Who do we think we are: Canada's reasonable
    (and less reasonable) accommodation debates